PUBLICATIONS OF THE INSTITUTE OF HIGHER EDUCATION

Copies of these reports may be obtained from the
Bureau of Publications, Teachers College, Columbia University

LIBERAL EDUCATION

and

BUSINESS

WILLIAM M. KEPHART

Wharton School of Finance and Commerce
University of Pennsylvania

JAMES E. McNULTY

Wharton School of Finance and Commerce
University of Pennsylvania

AND

EARL J. McGRATH

Executive Officer
Institute of Higher Education

PUBLISHED FOR THE

INSTITUTE OF HIGHER EDUCATION

BY THE

BUREAU OF PUBLICATIONS

TEACHERS COLLEGE, COLUMBIA UNIVERSITY

FOREWORD

IN 1956 THE INSTITUTE OF HIGHER EDUCATION LAUNCHED A SERIES
of inquiries into the curricula of undergraduate professional schools.
These analyses were focussed principally on the balance between
the professional and liberal studies included in each of these programs which typically prepare young people for the practice of one
of the professions. The original plan included a study of a representative group of undergraduate schools of business administration.
Indeed, Professors William M. Kephart and James E. McNulty of
the Wharton School at the University of Pennsylvania, at the invita-
tion of the Institute, conducted an inquiry into the literature dealing
with the historical development of, and the current opinions concerning, the liberal and professional components in the curricula of
schools of business. The Executive Officer of the Institute of Higher
Education, simultaneously began visits to a number of such institutions to make direct observations on their curricular policies and
structures.

As these various activities progressed, however, two much more
comprehensive and detailed studies of schools of business were
initiated with large support from the Carnegie Corporation of New
York and the Fund for the Advancement of Education. The results
were published in 1959 under the titles *Higher Education for
Business* (by Robert A. Gordon and James E. Howell) and *The
Education of American Businessmen* (by Frank C. Pierson). The
publication of these reports seemed to make unnecessary at that time

the related inquiry of the Institute. Consequently, activities in the field of education for business were temporarily halted and the materials which had already been assembled on the subject were retained for later consideration and possible publication.

Since the issuance of the reports in 1959 the various branches of the profession concerned with education for business have been discussing the recommendations made and a number of persons have also made public statements on the issues involved. Many institutions have in the interim altered their courses of study. Professors John J. Clark and Blaise J. Opulente recently undertook a review of some of the changes in policies and practices in schools of business which have occurred in the past several years and other studies have been made within institutions of their own purposes and programs.

In view of the passage of time since the completion of the two studies in 1959 and the continued discussion of the objectives of education for business occupations it now seems timely to publish some of the Institute's materials originally prepared on this subject and recently brought up-to-date. It also seemed profitable to make a critical analysis of some of the intervening discussions in the hope of arriving at a further clarification of issues and if possible of establishing the emerging lines of development. The Institute was encouraged to make such a reassessment specifically for a meeting of the National Organization of the Council for Professional Education for Business in Pittsburgh, on December 27, 1962, and after this meeting the constituent supporting professional associations urged the widest possible distribution of the material bearing on the subject.

Accordingly, this monograph has now been prepared. It includes several chapters, which, though varied in their content and occasionally in point of view, are all related to the subject of the preparation of business personnel for their occupational duties. The first chapter, prepared by Earl J. McGrath, like counterparts in other Institute monographs on the professions, considers certain general problems common to all in their efforts to adjust their current educational programs to the changing conditions of American life.

Chapters 2 through 7, authored by Professors Kephart and McNulty, provide a historical review of the development of the curriculum from the early days of business education in the United States and critical analyses of the positions taken through the years and currently by those who have advocated a broader, more liberal curriculum for the preparation of business men and women. The last chapter, which—in another form—constituted the address prepared for the meeting in December 1962, attempts to review changing curricular patterns and practices in schools of business education and to evaluate them in terms of the evolving conditions in the American business enterprise and in life in general in this country. And, finally, there is an annotated bibliography, brought up-to-date in May 1963, for the benefit of the reader who wishes to make a more comprehensive study of the entire subject, or of any of its many related branches.

To a degree, different points of view are presented in the different chapters with regard to current practices in business education and the issues involved. These differences result not only from the fact that several authors are involved. They stem from the varying views which still widely prevail among those concerned with education for business and indeed among representatives of education for all the other professional occupations. There are still many unresolved problems in these various fields as there are in business. Yet consensus is being reached on some basic matters which were formerly vigorously debated. This publication is issued in the conviction that all those concerned should be currently informed about the changing views of leaders in business education concerning the purposes, content, and structure of the curriculum. Only through continued experimentation, evaluation, and public discussion will a larger consensus be reached on the important matters discussed in this publication.

The Executive Officer of the Institute wishes to thank the Carnegie Corporation of New York for the support which made this publication possible. He also wishes to express his gratitude to Professors Kephart and McNulty who not only made a scholarly contribution to the report, but also patiently waited for its delayed publication. Thanks are also due many deans and teachers in schools of business, especially Dean Charles E. Gilliland of Temple University's School of Business and Public Administration and Thomas L. Norton, former dean at New York University School of Commerce, Accounts, and Finance, whose interests have been continuous and vital since the inception of the project.

EARL J. McGRATH
Executive Officer

CONTENTS

Chapter 1

PROFESSIONAL EDUCATION FOR THE SECOND HALF OF THE TWENTIETH CENTURY*

THE EVENTS OF THE PAST SEVERAL YEARS HAVE SHARPLY FOCUSED attention on the purposes and the functions of American higher education. Stimulated by the advances in science and technology in other parts of the world, educators and laymen have become particularly concerned with the merits of professional and technological education on the one hand and liberal studies on the other, and even more with the relationships which should obtain between them.

The questions involved are ancient. In the fourth century B.C., Aristotle, commenting on the educational principles and practices of his time, said: ". . . the existing practice [of education] is perplexing; no one knows on what principle it should proceed—should the useful in life, or should virtue, or should higher knowledge, be the aim of our training; all three opinions have been entertained. Again, about the means there is no agreement."[1] Ever since those ancient days partisans of two main types of education—often called "professional" and "liberal"—have defended their respective merits. The debate continues today with renewed vigor, and for a number of reasons it is timely.

First, the general public is agitated by Russian advances in the

---

*By Earl J. McGrath. The ideas in this chapter have been considerably elaborated and expanded in *Liberal Education in the Professions,* by Earl J. McGrath (New York: Bureau of Publications, Teachers College, Columbia University, 1959).

[1] Aristotle, *Politics* (New York: The Modern Library, 1943), p. 321.

1

fields of science and technology. Many Americans are raising questions about the reasons for what they rightly or wrongly consider to be the superiority of the Russians in the type of education basic to their startling achievements in the sciences. Although the issues involved in these questions extend far beyond the boundaries of higher education, some of the more urgent problems as seen by many educators and thoughtful laymen are related to the functions and programs of colleges and universities.

Those who advocate an intensification of education in the professional and semiprofessional vocations and in the fields of scholarship concerned with science have the onerous responsibility of describing how preparation for the other broad activities of life is to be adequately provided. Those, on the contrary, who stress the social and personal values of liberal education must realistically face the increasing need in the modern world for persons with advanced training in an occupational field—and show how this is to be furnished in increasing measure. The significance of occupational education can be appreciated only when it is realized that there are now twenty-two hundred occupations requiring highly trained manpower, and that ten to twenty more are created annually. As valuable as liberal arts education may be, it is not all that is needed by those employed in the specialized vocations. It is necessary and reasonable, therefore, to reconsider the full complement of educational services these workers must have if they are to be vocationally efficient and civically competent.

Second, for several decades the proportion of all college students attending professional units in colleges and universities has steadily mounted. Many of the present schools, such as those in business administration and journalism, were inconspicuous, if not completely missing, in the total enterprise of higher education at the turn of the century. There were, for example, only three schools of business before 1900 and these enrolled a mere handful of students. Now tens of thousands of students attend several hundred such institutions. The growth of the college and university divisions devoted to the various forms of education directly related to an occupation is evident from the enrollments in these institutions. Dael Wolfle has shown that in 1901, of all the first degrees granted, the aggregate of those in business, agriculture, education, and engineering was only 4.1 per cent of the total awarded by all types of institutions.[2] By 1951–1953, however, the figure had risen to 46.4 per cent, or almost half the first degrees awarded. If these students are to receive any education other than that which prepares them for their occupational activities, this general education must in some manner or other be made an integral part of the professional program. There are many issues in this merging of two sets of educational objectives which deserve thoughtful analysis on the basis of which systematic planning can take place.

Third, although the series of questions involved in establishing the proper proportions and relationships between the professional and the liberal education of college-going youth most obviously apply to the universities, those queries must also be answered by the faculties of liberal arts colleges. These older units in our system of higher education, like their sister institutions, have in the past several decades inaugurated a wide variety of professional and semi-professional curricula. Another study conducted by the Institute of Higher Education[3] has revealed that some independent liberal arts colleges offer more than twenty vocationally oriented programs leading to one or another bachelor's degree, and that virtually all such institutions provide some instruction of this type. Moreover, the specialization in the various conventional liberal arts departments has now become so intense that to all intents and purposes these programs are no less vocational than their counterparts in schools of engineering, business administration, and education. If, therefore, the graduates of the liberal arts colleges are to leave these institutions adequately prepared to live intelligently and effectively in the larger sphere of life outside their occupation, the same questions which are matters of consideration in the separate professional schools must be raised concerning the relationship between general and specialized education in the liberal arts colleges.

Fourth, there is increasing concern among our citizens about the

[2] Dael Wolfle, *America's Resources of Specialized Talent* (New York: Harper and Brothers, 1954), p. 292.

[3] Earl J. McGrath and Charles H. Russell, *Are Liberal Arts Colleges Becoming Professional Schools?* (New York: Bureau of Publications, Teachers College, Columbia University, 1958).

rising cost of higher education in money and in time. Medical education is the prime example of the steady lengthening of the course of formal study and the consequent increase of the financial burden on the student and his family. As late as 1900 young men could enter a medical school with no more than a secondary schooling and complete the medical course in two academic years. Now the average for premedical and medical education is eight years, to which are added varying but usually long periods of internship or residency.

In some schools of education, nursing, pharmacy, and commerce, and in other professional fields as well, formal education has been extended to five or six years. Serious social problems are involved in the steady extension of pre-employment education. There are curtailments of earning capacity, maladjustments in personal and family life, and an often unrecognized selection of individuals whose parents are in the social and economic groups which can afford the large capital investment required to complete a long professional course of study. This investigation is only tangentially concerned with these latter matters. It is, however, directly concerned with the related question as to whether a more carefully considered plan for the total education of the individual, involving a clarification of the purposes and character of both liberal and professional education, could not keep the scope of higher education within more reasonable and defensible bounds.

Finally, the opportunities for adult education now provided by almost all institutions of higher education, and the opportunities for continuing education of high quality within commerce and industry, make necessary a re-examination of the amount and kind of higher education a prospective practitioner needs before he enters upon his intended life work. Considering the wealth of postgraduate educational opportunities now available, all baccalaureate curricula, both those in professional schools and in liberal arts colleges, require critical reappraisal aimed at determining as objectively as possible which educational functions can most properly be performed before graduation and which can most profitably be conducted after the individual actually assumes his vocational responsibilities. A review of these matters again requires a reconsideration of the relationships between the various types of instruction now offered in undergraduate programs which too often operate under the fallacious assumption that the student's education does and necessarily must conclude on the day of graduation.

These, then, are the chief reasons for the present study of the curricula of selected undergraduate professional units in colleges and universities. Before undertaking the detailed analyses of various institutional policies and practices which constitute the major purpose of this study, it was necessary to explore the meaning and purpose of liberal and professional studies and to establish a working basis for properly interrelating these two educational functions in an integrated whole.

In considering a desirable pre-employment higher education for vocational competence, one must begin with the assumption that such education is necessary and desirable in the United States today. To some this suggestion may appear obvious and fruitless. Yet many educators and laymen question the whole concept of undergraduate education as preparation for earning a living except insofar as general, nonvocational instruction may be considered to provide that preparation. They would be satisfied with, or even prefer, either no training other than that provided on the job, or a formal vocational education beginning at the postbaccalaureate level. Such a concept is unrealistic because of the over-all purposes of higher education in our democratic society with its increasingly complicated economic structure and its mounting demands for higher education for individuals of ever more varied abilities, interests, and vocational objectives.

If the existence of undergraduate professional schools is justified, there can be no question that they must prepare students for their prospective work in a particular family of occupations. If the baccalaureate curriculum in commerce, for example, is not related to the activities of business enterprise, its existence per se cannot be justified. Some of those who have analyzed the need for education for business, and for other vocations as well, have advocated programs of studies so general that the *raison d'être* of a school of commerce is denied by the very breadth and the remoteness from business activities of the studies they recommend. Such proposals really deny the need for specialized education, or at least reserve it for graduate study or on-the-job training.

Even if such views were defensible in the abstract, they are unrealistic. The undergraduate professional units of our colleges and universities are firmly established in the academic structure and in the minds of our people. They are here to stay. They will be augmented by others in the years ahead. Enrollment trends in institutions of higher education show that undergraduates in professional schools increasingly outnumber those in liberal arts colleges. Hence, the meaningful question to be asked about the professional schools is how their offerings can be patterned to meet the needs of youth who have at least a tentative vocational objective but whose education must be so designed as to prepare them to act as intelligently in the broader contexts of life as in their own work.

A review of the emerging characteristics of the American economy and the history of higher education supplies convincing evidence that the number and the variety of baccalaureate programs with a specific occupational orientation will inevitably increase. It is important, therefore, that steps be taken now to justify the assumption that undergraduate professional schools will have both vocational and general objectives, and that these aims will be clearly reflected in the structure and the content of the curriculum. The compelling responsibility of those who determine the character and substance of undergraduate professional education is to design curricula which prepare the individual concurrently for a specialized calling and for the other varied activities of life. At first sight these broad purposes might appear to be visionary and unattainable within the normal four- or five-year period. If, however, only clearly comprehended and essential purposes control curriculum planning, and if all instruction which does not manifestly contribute toward the attainment of these twin objectives is cut away, a defensible program can be designed. The success of such an effort will, however, be dependent upon the acceptance of the basic principle that the professional course of study ought to be a whole in which traditional liberal arts instruction and the technical courses related to a particular occupation are joined to provide the full and relevant higher education appropriate to the needs of our times.

Before considering the matters of fact and theory which are germane to a discussion of the structure and content of professional undergraduate education, it should be observed that in an earlier

day much of the education in this country in all professional call-
ings was narrowly technical. Most curricula in that day and indeed
up to very recent times emphasized handbook information and rule-
of-thumb procedures while neglecting basic theory and generalized
knowledge useful in the infinitely varied circumstances of every-
day practice. This kind of training was in fact *illiberal* in terms of
any modern definition of either liberal or professional education.
But this exclusive purpose of earlier professional programs—to
make the individual technically competent—has now been largely
replaced in theory if not in practice by the conception that all specialties must rest on a solid basis of theoretical knowledge and be
practiced with the imaginative employment of general intellectual
skills.

The most advanced views today assume that, if it is to be fully
effective in preparing graduates for the complicated demands of
contemporary life, professional education must have not a single
goal but rather three comprehensive objectives. First, because of
its very nature, it must obviously inculcate the corpus of knowledge,
the complement of skills, and the traits of personality and character
which constitute the distinctive features of a particular craft. It is
these characteristics which give the profession its cohesiveness and
identity. The celebrated psychologist William James, who, in his
monumental *Principles of Psychology,* analyzed the attributes which
differentiate one occupation from others, observed that "Already
at the age of twenty-five you see the professional mannerism settling
down on the young commercial traveler, on the young doctor, on
the young minister, on the counselor-at-law." At one time, cultivating these distinguishing qualities of an occupational group was
the sole purpose of its entire preparatory educational program. Today, however, at least the more forward-looking institutions consider two other aims as hardly less significant than that of equip-
ping the student to perform effectively the duties of his chosen work.

A second purpose, and one of rising importance, is concerned
with the general education which all those who attend an institution
of higher education must have if they are to understand, and to live
competently in, an increasingly complex democratic society. President John Hannah of Michigan State University expressed this

8   *Liberal Education and Business*

newer conception when he told representatives of the land-grant colleges that "It is not enough that our young people be outstanding technicians. The first and never-forgotten objective must be that every product of our educational system must be given that training that will enable him to be an effective citizen, appreciating his opportunities and fully willing to assume his responsibilities in a great democracy."[4] Intelligent living today requires a knowledge of matters of domestic and international affairs infinitely more complicated and shifting than those of even a generation ago. Moreover, recent advances in the physical and biological sciences impinge so directly on the life of the average citizen that he cannot live capably today in ignorance of these arresting penetrations of the unknown regions of the physical world. The rapid growth of reliable knowledge in the physical and the social sciences requires that the purposes of higher education for a vocation be extended beyond the bounds of technical knowledge or expertness in his own field.

Furthermore, an educational institution can hardly absolve itself of a third responsibility—that of assisting the student in gaining self-understanding, a moral grounding, and a consistent view of the world. In the words of the Committee on Aims and Scope of Engineering Education, the humanities and the social sciences have a responsibility to assist the student in the "development of moral, ethical, and social welfare and to a sound professional attitude."[5] Though a graduate may be ever so competent a practitioner and citizen, without knowledge of his own nature and a reasoned philosophy of life, he will fail to realize his full potential. Throughout his adult life the kaleidoscopic world around him will remain a meaningless flux of unrelated events. Recognizing the need for this philosophical orientation, many leaders in professional education appraise it as highly as professional skill and civic competence. In fact, one leader lists these three dominant purposes of journalism

[4] John A. Hannah, "The Place of the Land-Grant College in the Public Educational System of the Future," *Proceedings of the 58th Annual Convention of the Association of Land-Grant Colleges and Universities,* Vol. 58 (1944), p. 76.

[5] Society for the Promotion of Engineering Education, Committee on Aims and Scope of Engineering Education, "Report," *Journal of Engineering Education,* Vol. 30 (March 1940), p. 564.

education in the following order: "(1) It should fit the student for being an effective citizen. (2) It should fit him for living a useful, full, satisfying life. (3) It should provide basic preparation for work in journalism."[6]

If these three comprehensive objectives of professional education are to be achieved, a judicious readjustment must be made in the balance of instruction directly related to the student's prospective occupation and instruction in the disciplines traditionally termed "the liberal arts and sciences." Before considering what types of readjustments are necessary, however, consideration must be given to the purposes of liberal arts education in order to determine to what extent and by what means they can be served in the curricula of professional schools.

What are the major purposes of liberal education in contemporary American society? Though it would doubtless be difficult, if not impossible, to arrive at a generally acceptable definition of liberal education, perhaps a measure of agreement can be reached through a description of the types of abilities and personality traits which liberal education might be expected to engender in those who have been subject to its influence.

First, it would probably be generally agreed that those who have had a liberal education should have acquired a broad knowledge of the various major areas of learning—the natural sciences, the social sciences, and the humanities, including the fine arts. Though it is doubtless true, as Whitehead observed, that "A merely well-informed man is the most useless bore on God's earth," it is no less true that today the ignorant are a menace to themselves and to their fellow citizens. No person can now live fully and effectively, according to Ortega y Gasset, without at least a modest knowledge of "the culture, the vital system of ideas, which the age has attained" —and Ortega meant the age in which the individual is living.

Yet it must be apparent to anyone who moves among "educated" people that some who leave our institutions of higher education today are unacquainted with the living ideas of their time. Haltingly they feel their way in darkness through many of the com-

[6]Leslie G. Moeller, "Goals of Professional Education for Journalism," *The Quill,* Vol. 40 (August 1952), pp. 6 ff.

mon avenues of life because their path is unilluminated by even the
most elementary knowledge of many aspects of their own being or
of the physical and social universe which surrounds them. That
many who have spent four or more years in an institution of higher
education are innocent of much of the reliable knowledge of their
time is attested by the experiences of the author of a best-seller on
the social implications of atomic energy. In discussions with college audiences he observed that on many matters of fundamental
significance they were no better informed and hardly more curious
than the man in the street.

In view of the enormous mass and accelerating rate of growth
of knowledge, students cannot fairly be expected to encompass any
large portion of it in four, or even in forty, years. They can, however, properly be expected to gain an acquaintance with the basic
facts and principles of the various disciplines. A student who com-
pletes a professional education of four or more years with however
distinguished a record in engineering, pharmacy, education, or agriculture, but with little or no knowledge of English literature, history, philosophy, or economics, is not liberally educated. He will
be prepared to think and act effectively neither in his chosen occupation nor in the many life situations which are the common lot
of all.

The mere possession of facts, however, does not guarantee the
efficient, the incisive, and the imaginative use of the mind. Cardinal
Newman, in his celebrated analysis of the nature of liberal education, *The Idea of a University,* has said:

> Knowledge then is the indispensable condition of expansion of mind
> and the instrument of attaining to it; this cannot be denied, it is ever
> to be insisted on; I begin with it as a first principle; however, the very
> truth of it carries men too far . . . the end of a Liberal Education is
> not mere knowledge.[7]

Second, then, liberal education ought to cultivate those skills
and habits of reasoning which constitute intellectual competence,
the capacity to think logically and clearly, the ability to organize
one's thoughts on the varied subjects with which the citizen today

[7] John Henry Newman, *The Idea of a University* (New York: Longmans, Green
and Co., 1955), p. 115.

must unavoidably concern himself. In a sentence, these faculties might collectively be described as the capacity to order and interpret a complex set of circumstances in the physical, social, or artistic world, and to bring one's full intellectual resources skillfully to bear on the solution of a problem.

Just as the student must have some knowledge of many fields, so also, in order to gain competence in using the diverse forms of reasoning, he must have experience with intellectual processes other than those conventionally employed in his major academic field of interest. The various disciplines do, of course, employ some intellectual processes in common—the logical deduction of conclusions from valid premises, for example—whether the matter under consideration involves the facts of science, history, or art. Yet they also use intellectual methodologies in part peculiar to themselves. The chemist or physicist will only be satisfied with knowledge in which the probability of error is reduced to negligible proportions, while the historian or the sociologist, dealing as he does with human acts and events, must be satisfied with a much greater range of error of both fact and judgment. The student of art enjoys much greater freedom of subjective evaluation and interpretation than either the physical or the social scientist, but the intellectual processes by which he deals with reality are no less important than those employed by other disciplines.

The most distinctive and yet the most widely used processes of reasoning are doubtless the deductive method of formal logic and the inductive method of science. Those who are to be liberally educated can gain familiarity with these mental processes and skill in their use most readily by the study of mathematics and the sciences. No person can live intelligently today unless he understands the methods of reasoning with which scientists have so dramatically explored the unknown regions of the universe, from the boundless oceans of cosmic space to the infinitesimal region of the atom's nucleus. The intellectual procedures used in the conception of a hypothesis, the arrangement of an experiment to test it, the drawing of conclusions from the facts thus established—all these skills every citizen needs to acquire if he is to reason validly and objectively about physical phenomena. Moreover, properly taught, these habits of thought can be broadly applied in analyses of the complex social world with which all human beings are surrounded. Since the sciences differ in their use of these procedures with a wide variety of physical problems, the broadest range of acquaintance with these subjects will accomplish the fullest understanding and skill in the use of their methods.

Other branches of learning, the humanistic disciplines for example, use somewhat different intellectual operations in their interpretation of the world and the activities of men. Though they naturally employ the laws of logic in constructing a reasoned view of reality, their distinctive characteristic is their concern with values, with the ends of life, with the destiny of man. Those who teach history, literature, foreign languages, philosophy, and the arts cannot confine themselves to a consideration of the characteristics and behavior of exactly measurable phenomena. They must introduce the student to the reflections of creative minds on the nature of man and his world and their conclusions which are usually couched in much less precise terms than those of the scientist. The concern of teachers of these subjects must be with man, not as a physico-chemical complex within a mechanistically determined system, but rather as a being of purposes, values, loves, hates, and ideals—and sometimes as a seer or prophet with divine inspiration. In literature, the student should vicariously enjoy many of the richest experiences of life, gaining insight into human motivation and behavior attainable in no other way except through personal experience.

Still another area of human intellectual endeavor uses somewhat different approaches in its interpretation of reality. The social sciences—economics, sociology, and political science, for example—insofar as possible follow scientific procedure by constructing hypotheses, setting up experimental controls, and making accurate observations. These disciplines also use other investigative procedures, including statistical method, historical analysis, and case studies. Unlike the natural scientist, however, the scholar concerned with social phenomena often cannot arrange experiments which others can repeat. On the contrary, he must sometimes accept data of unprovable authenticity or of incomplete representativeness and, reasoning cautiously, arrive at tentative conclusions. Much of his material does not lend itself to the exact measurement used by the physical scientist. In the words of Taussig, one of this country's most celebrated economists, the social scientist is concerned with the "wavering and incalculable behavior" of man. The educated person must be skilled in these processes of tentative and precise reasoning about phenomena of inexact measurement. Most human actions must be based on evidence which, though not fully conclusive, is the best available at the time. One of the chief aims of higher education should be to cultivate habits which will prevent human beings from acting blindly, with no facts, and also from procrastinating indefinitely because the last shred of evidence is not in.

The liberally educated mind possesses another set of intellectual abilities, those involving the effective use of the various symbols and media of expression and communication. In the formulation of concepts and in the orderly development of a reasoned view of life, the meanings of words are the building blocks; the logical relationships among these verbal expressions, the cement which holds them together. No aspect of higher education has been more severely criticized than the teaching of the skills of communication. Yet instruction in this subject is highly valued by those who realize its importance in all phases of adult life. Several years ago this statement was well documented in a study of over thirteen thousand degree-holding employees of the General Electric Company. These graduates were divided into two groups, those who had attended engineering schools and those who were graduates from nonengineering curricula, mainly liberal arts colleges. When asked to appraise the various subjects they had pursued in undergraduate days in terms of their career value, the nonengineers placed English communication, both oral and written, at the top of the list, and this subject was placed second only to mathematics by the engineering graduates.[8] The symbols of mathematics and of the arts, though not as widely and as frequently used by the ordinary citizen as words, are nevertheless essential elements in the lives of cultured men and women.

[8] "What They Think of Their Higher Education, A Report of a Survey of the Opinions of 13,586 College Graduates, Employees of the General Electric Company," *Educational Relations Bulletin* (January 1957).

Equipped with essential knowledge and the skills of intellectual workmanship, the college graduate may nevertheless have failed to reach another important goal, perhaps the *sine qua non* of liberal education. Though richly informed, and capable of clear and cogent reasoning, he may yet be intolerant, unwise, intellectually stagnant, and inept in the arts of human association. The *third* major objective of liberal education is, therefore, concerned with attitudes, ideals, and traits of personality and character. These qualities, harder to describe and to measure than the other outcomes of liberal education, are yet the hallmark of the liberally educated person. As has been said, they are the qualities that remain after all the facts which were learned have been forgotten.

The liberally educated person embraces certain values. He has at least a provisionally formed and examined philosophy of life, a *Weltanschauung,* a religion around which he organizes the varied purposes and activities of his existence. These values of the liberally educated man represent not only the ideas and causes for which he would live, but more importantly those for which if necessary he would die. They give stability to his being. They serve to keep the ship of life steady on course as it is buffeted by the unpredictable forces of man and of nature. Without them the lives of men have no direction, for, as Socrates said, "If a man does not know to what port he is sailing, no wind is favorable."

Knowing his limitations, the liberally educated man has respect for the rights and views of others. He is humble, not only before the capricious and uncontrollable forces of nature, but also in the presence of his own ignorance. And most important of all, he continually seeks wisdom through the extension of his knowledge and reflection on its meanings. Realizing how much he does not know, he is driven by an unrelenting curiosity, an unquenchable thirst for deeper knowledge and fuller understanding. Unless professional education inspires the desire to learn, to extend the scope of one's knowledge, to increase one's insights into the nature of things, it has condemned its recipients to eventual ignorance and mental stagnation. For the explosive increase of knowledge is the most arresting fact in today's world of learning, and swiftly accelerating change the most characteristic feature of modern life.

Even if higher education were able to supply each student with all the knowledge needed to understand the world in which he currently lives, and even if it could sharpen the intellectual skills to a fine point, it would have failed if it had not added to these achievements the inculcation of the irresistible desire to learn and to know. For as knowledge grows and the world changes, all who wish to live intelligently must continue to grow and to change through learning. Unless education initiates a chain reaction in which each advance in understanding sets off the desire for greater growth in wisdom, those who leave our campuses will soon reach a state of permanent intellectual rest. They will lose touch with the ongoing world.

The purposes and character of professional education require a similarly intensive and critical analysis. Since, however, the remainder of this volume is concerned with a review of the attitudes of faculty members and administrative officers, and of the practices in selected institutions with respect to this matter, only general guide lines for the development of a professional curriculum will be suggested at this point.

The dominant principle to be applied in determining the character and content of an undergraduate professional program has to do with the degree of specialization the curriculum may be expected to provide. The substance of a professional course of study, and the manner in which it is organized and presented, must be decided in terms of the vast bulk of modern knowledge, its rate of growth and change, the time available to the average student for pre-employment training, and especially the proper purposes of initial education in a vocation. As these various factors which irresistibly shape professional education are analyzed, the dominant principle in curriculum construction is thrown into high relief. It becomes axiomatic that the student can be, and in principle should be, given only enough basic specialized instruction related to a vocational field to qualify him for initial gainful employment. W. Earl Armstrong sets forth this controlling idea in relation to teacher education, for example, when he says:

> It is not assumed that the pre-service curriculum should attempt to provide all of the insights and skills that the teacher will need in order to be a fully competent person. Rather, the function of the pre-serv-

ice curriculum as here assumed is to provide the best possible preparation for the teacher to *begin* to teach. A pre-service curriculum based on this assumption will of necessity leave all aspects of the teacher's education incomplete. That is to say, the general education of the teacher will need further strengthening, the area or areas of subject-matter concentration will need either further broadening or deepening, and further additions will need to be made to the professional insights and skills of the teacher.[9]

If the several values in a professional curriculum are to be kept in proper balance, the student cannot be prepared as an expert in any specific job. Undergraduate instruction can be expected to do no more than acquaint him with the vocabulary and the basic principles of a broad field such as pharmacy, engineering, or nursing, and cultivate the intellectual skills by means of which new knowlelge can be acquired and applied to the infinitely varying problems of day-to-day practice. This conception of the scope of a professional school's purposes has been well expressed by Dean Helen Nahm of the School of Nursing at the University of California:

> I think our major problem in a professional school . . . is that we must, in a period of time which seems reasonable to students and their parents, prepare both a liberally educated person and a person with competencies essential for beginning practice in a professional field.

Cogent reasons support the view that an undergraduate professional curriculum should embrace only those learning experiences necessary to orient the student broadly in his chosen occupation without aiming to cultivate a high degree of competence in any of its specialized branches.

The store of detailed knowledge in any professional field is enormous, and it expands prodigiously. This accelerating growth of fact and theory, the invariable characteristic of every intellectual realm, explains why no one can become or remain a genuine expert in a specialized branch of learning except by long years of study and by continually renewed acquaintance with evolving fact, principle, technique, and practice. It is for this reason that even those who, for example, graduate from a school of business administra-

9 W. Earl Armstrong, "The Teacher Education Curriculum," *The Journal of Teacher Education*, Vol. 8, No. 3 (September 1957), p. 232.

tion with distinction and with the beginning of a specialization in management or retailing are nevertheless given positions relatively low in the structure of a business enterprise.

Second, highly specialized undergraduate instruction fails to reach its reputed goal because each set of circumstances in professional life has its own peculiar structure. To a degree it involves concepts and techniques which vary from those of all other situations. Consequently, the principles of accounting, orchestration, *materia medica,* or educational psychology must be adapted to the special circumstances and needs of a particular situation. The beginner who takes up his duties in any profession prepared to apply a specific body of detailed facts or procedures to new sets of circumstances will find his bag of tricks hopelessly inadequate. Unfortunately, he will only then belatedly realize that in concentrating excessively on a narrow specialty he has failed to gain the flexibility of mind and personality required to understand and to deal effectively with a host of important matters both professional and otherwise. Inevitably he will lack breadth in both general and professional knowledge and in the intellectual skills essential to their profitable use in the varied patterns of professional exigencies.

In the making of a professional curriculum, another guiding principle is related to the technical courses themselves. Those who have considered the matter most studiously are convinced that *even professional instruction* should stress broad principles, key ideas, and overarching generalizations rather than detailed facts or techniques. Here it is profitable to raise questions concerning what kind of education is of most worth, and how much can be accomplished in the time available.

The curricula of forward-looking engineering schools, for example, provide convincing illustrations of successful efforts to place greater emphasis on principles than on techniques, thus making possible the enlargement of the general education component and a broader orientation in the vocational field itself. Even in the engineering subjects many schools have adopted a core program of professional subject matter as the common basis of the specialties such as civil, chemical, electrical, and mechanical engineering. The enlargement of these common components has been possible only through the dropping of some specialized instruction which in earlier years pre-empted a considerable portion of the four-year curriculum. This shift in emphasis has increased the student's knowledge of theoretical engineering and of the liberal arts disciplines, thus enhancing both his occupational and his civic competence.

Another principle to be applied in designing a professional course of study relates to the cultivation of attitudes and motivations which are not the sole concern of any subject-matter field, but rather the responsibility of all. Proposals for the reconstruction of professional curricula will succeed or fail largely to the extent that students are helped to recognize undergraduate education as only the beginning rather than the end of a long process of personal growth. Unless the experiences of the college years are viewed in this light the student is likely to misconceive the aims of higher education. Not uncommonly, faculty members and curriculum makers encourage students' misconceptions of the purposes and the potential of undergraduate education. A subconscious feeling, subtly transferred to those under instruction, that they must "learn it now or never" is the origin of the common compulsion to include every last bit of information, to explore every remote corner of the subject, in a single course. Under the influence of this point of view all curricula have become swollen with masses of dispensable facts, and the atmosphere of the classroom has become one of hurried absorption of facts rather than of reflective analysis and the orderly expansion of mind.

A curriculum with the proper objectives ought to provide the basic experiences needed by the neophyte to begin his practice with a sufficient body of knowledge to give him confidence in his own ability and to make possible further professional growth through individual study, practice, and additional part-time instruction in so-called "refresher" courses. He ought to have the flexibility of mind to pursue and to accept additions to knowledge and innovations in procedures as they appear. He ought also to have a vision of the wider significance of his work in the whole social context of his time. More than this an undergraduate program cannot and need not be expected to accomplish.

The achievement of these two sets of purposes for a responsible and full life as a private citizen and as a member of an occupational group is an ambitious undertaking. Yet, under proper conditions it is not an unrealistic goal. Our national and personal welfare demand that it be reached within the next decade; our needs for highly skilled workers and for informed and active citizens are patently urgent.

If these aims are to be realized, however, certain of the presently controlling ideas and practices in American higher education require reassessment. Many of the graduates of institutions of higher education will not reach these goals if it is assumed that only those disciplines commonly classified under the caption "liberal arts" have these desiderata as their aims. On the contrary, much of the instruction in professional curricula such as engineering, business administration, education, and nursing must be expected (as it already lives up to the expectation in some places) to cultivate the qualities of mind and character often considered the exclusive province of the liberal arts.

No one has better described the possibility of achieving the ends of liberal education through the study of specialized subjects than President Virgil M. Hancher of the State University of Iowa, who at a meeting of the Association of Land-Grant Colleges and Universities in 1953 said:

> We forget that it is possible to become liberally educated by the teaching and study of professional or specialized subjects in a liberal manner. . . .
>
> While in general I would support the proposition that there are some things which every liberally educated man should know, I fear that we have been led into error sometimes by believing that the study of certain subject matter inevitably results in a liberal education. This is a doubtful proposition. It is nearer to the truth to say that there is no subject matter, worthy of a place in the curriculum of a modern Land-Grant College or state university, which cannot be taught either as a professional specialty or as a liberal subject.[10]

It is obvious that courses in engineering or pharmacy, if properly taught, acquaint the student with a wide range of scientific facts and cultivate the intellectual skills of the scientist. They also instill a respect for truth, a humbleness of spirit, a desire to learn, and the habit of philosophical reflection about the place of man in a limitless cos-

[10] Virgil M. Hancher, "Liberal Education in Professional Curricula," *Proceedings of the Sixty-Seventh Convention of the American Association of Land-Grant Colleges and State Universities,* Vol. 67 (1953), p. 45.

mos. The same can be said for instruction in other professional programs, though the emphasis on particular subject matter and skills would obviously vary with the field concerned.

Engineering can be used to illustrate how a rounded education can be provided for the student in a professional course of study. The first objective of liberal education, acquainting the student with the fundamental facts and principles in the three main areas of knowledge, can be accomplished by supplementing the basic courses in science with instruction in the social sciences, the humanities, and the skills of communication. The requirements in the social sciences and the humanities ought to be met by the pursuit of courses especially designed to bring the student into touch with the leading principles and the key ideas in a broad range of subjects not included in courses in engineering and basic science.

In the social sciences, for example, such subjects might include history, political science, sociology, and economics. Courses should be unlike conventional elementary courses in that no attempt should be made to cover all the detailed knowledge necessary for advanced study. Instead, selected special topics ought to be studied intensively, so that the study would emphasize relationships between the constituent disciplines, and inculcate skill in the use of the methods of thought employed in dealing with social problems. Thus the second objective of cultivating intellectual skills in the social sciences would be accomplished. Comparable instruction in literature, languages, philosophy, and the arts should acquaint the student with the content and methods of the humanities. Since scientific subjects are necessarily basic to specialized engineering courses, it could be assumed that all students would have gained a considerable knowledge of science and skill in the use of its methods.

The third objective of liberal education, that of cultivating the attitudes and the traits of character which signalize the liberally educated mind, must necessarily be the responsibility of all teachers of all subjects. Any subject can be taught so as to increase the student's respect for truth and for the worth of the individual, his appreciation of his own smallness in our vast universe, and his love of wisdom and desire to learn. For this reason, as Hancher holds, courses of study cannot on the basis of content or method alone be classified as liberal or not liberal. Instruction in a professional school which aims to achieve these objectives may certainly be classified as liberal, and courses in colleges of liberal arts which do not have these aims can surely not be described as liberal.

The graduate of such a program in engineering would possess not only the knowledge of his world at large and the aptitude to use his intellectual resources in expanding his learning. He would be capable of seeing his own occupational activities in the larger social context of his time. Similar curricular arrangements are feasible in all other professional schools. The general principle of curriculum construction involved is that the two major areas of knowledge not basic to the professional subject matter be adequately represented by appropriate general instruction. In business administration, for example, these would be the humanities and the natural sciences; in agriculture, the social sciences and the humanities; in music, the natural and the social sciences; and so on for all the other professions.

Whether these broad purposes of liberal education will really be achieved will depend on the teachers. A course in finance, for example, taught with emphasis on general economic principles, with consideration for the historical development and the present importance of financial institutions in Western society, and with constant reference to the interrelationship of money and banking with the facts of sociology, anthropology, political science, and psychology, not to mention ethics and art, will have many of the values of liberal education, whatever its uses may be in educating a student for employment in the world of commerce. Conversely, a course in Greek literature with an emphasis on dates, literary style, linguistic analysis, and the esoteric subject matter of the teacher's research on some peculiar characteristic of Greek grammar, may produce few of the desirable results of liberal study. The teacher and the preparation he receives for his responsibilities in the classroom are, always have been, and always will be the decisive factor in liberal or, for that matter, any other kind of education. The present inadequacies in American higher education, particularly in its failure to preserve the heritage of liberal culture, have their origin in the attitudes, purposes, and skills of the teachers. Many teachers—whether in professional schools or liberal arts colleges—in their preoccupation with the cultivation of specialized knowledge and the techniques of their own chosen narrow field of intellectual activity, have lost sight of the more inclusive purposes of higher undergraduate education.

Professional schools which adopt a broader set of objectives and make the requisite changes in their practices to bring them into conformity with these principles will provide more fully that generous education required by this generation to live more intelligently in the complex contemporary world. They will contribute more fully to the enrichment and strengthening of this democratic society in which high production is of undeniable importance in peace and in war, but of no more pressing urgency or greater significance than informed citizenship and self-knowledge. As institutions generally adopt the pattern already in effect among the most enterprising, the ideal of education for high professional competence, for informed and active citizenship, and for a rich and integrated personal life will be within reach of all undergraduates in professional schools. It is to the realization of these ideals that these institutions might well dedicate themselves in this period when our people, with an eye to the ultimate destiny of our nation, are reassessing all of American education.

Chapter 2

HISTORY OF BUSINESS EDUCATION

COLLEGIATE EDUCATION IN THE UNITED STATES BEGAN AS A FUNCtion of the liberal arts college. In the colonial period most liberal arts colleges were affiliated with some religious denomination, and in good part the course offerings were designed to prepare young men for the ministry. As the nation expanded, and as the population increased, *specialized* collegiate education became a societal necessity. In consequence, the eighteenth and nineteenth centuries saw the establishment of medical schools, law schools, engineering schools, and the like.

One of the areas of American life that much later became the subject of specialized collegiate education was business. It was not until 1881 that the first collegiate business school—the University of Pennsylvania's Wharton School—was established, and for seventeen years the Wharton School stood as the lone pioneer. In 1898 business schools were established at the University of Chicago and the University of California, and in 1900 three more schools were added to the list—at Wisconsin, Dartmouth, and New York University. In the next twenty-five years the number of such schools was to grow rapidly, but as of the turn of the century the nation that was to become the showcase of capitalistic enterprise could boast only six collegiate schools of business.

There are two reasons for this apparent temporal lag in business education: In the first place, the very idea of specialized training in business met with resistance from the purveyors of traditional liberal arts education—a resistance which, as the following pages will show, has never fully disappeared. Second, collegiate business education, like other areas of specialized training, arose in response to a need, and this particular need did not manifest itself much before the close of the nineteenth century. Early American economy was basically agricultural in nature, and it was not until after the War of 1812 that the adumbrations of industrialization and corporate enterprise were felt. The nineteenth century witnessed a vast development of our natural resources, and an expansion of domestic markets. Population moved westward, transportation and communication facilities improved, cities grew in size and number, new forms of power were utilized, and machine production came to supplant much of the hand labor. As time passed, technological advances took place at an unprecedented rate, and mass production was made more and more efficient. By 1870 the concentration of industry was underway, a movement which was to eventuate in dozens of corporation giants. It was at this point—and not until this point—that the need for specialized collegiate training for business became evident. As Hofstadter and Hardy have pointed out:

> Clearly the emergence of the business school as a flourishing center of specialized training came on the heels of the bureaucratization of American business, which was a well-established trend by 1900) In the entrepreneurs' heyday of the mid-nineteenth century, when the characteristic form of business education was an apprenticeship in business, a collegiate business school would have been an incongruity. In this, an age of small business and new enterprises, the son of a small businessman, or of an entrepreneur who had built a large enterprise, was in a position to inherit ownership; and the man who aspired to start a new business was about as well off if he spent his later teens in actual business practice as he was if he spent these years in acquiring further formal education. With the development of the large corporation, however, and its increasing dominance in American economic life, business success was less indentifiable with ownership, more with a high managerial position. It was not possible for the managerial executive, as it had been for the owning executive, to pass on his social and business position to his son by simple inheritance . . . As the manager sought to promote and educate his heirs into positions of profit and power, he found higher education in

general, and business education in particular, to be increasingly useful.[1]

As the twentieth century got underway it was obvious that the day of the Large Corporation had not only arrived but was here to stay. As big business expanded, so did the need for business school graduates, and as a result collegiate schools of business grew both in number and in terms of student enrollment.

THE RISE OF THE BUSINESS SCHOOL

Although the University of Pennsylvania's Wharton School of Finance and Commerce was the first permanently established collegiate school of business, several unsuccessful attempts had been made at other schools. As early as 1851 the University of Louisiana had experimented with a school of commerce, and similar ventures were begun in 1866 at the University of Wisconsin, and in 1869 at Washington and Lee. However, since none of these experiments was successful, it remained for Joseph Wharton, well-known Philadelphia iron-master and financier, to provide the ideological and financial ($100,000) impetus which led to the establishment of the first successful collegiate business school. A firm believer in general as well as specialized (business) education, and imbued with the idea that all college training must be oriented toward citizenship, community responsibility, and high ethical standards, Wharton spelled out what he believed to be the proper objectives of a business school, among which were the following:

> To provide for young men special means of training and correct instruction in the knowledge and in the arts of modern finance and economy, both public and private, in order that, being well informed and free from delusions in these important subjects, they may either serve the community skillfully, as well as faithfully, in offices of trust, or, remaining in private life, they may prudently manage their own

[1] Richard Hofstadter and C. DeWitt Hardy, *The Development and Scope of Higher Education in the United States* (New York: Columbia University Press, 1952), pp. 90-91. See also Mabel Newcomer, *The Big Business Executive—The Factors That Made Him, 1900-1950* (New York: Columbia University Press, 1955).

affairs and aid in maintaining sound financial morality; in short, to establish means for imparting a liberal education in all matters concerning finance and economy.

In his "Project for a School of Finance and Economy to form a new Department of the University," the source of the above quotation (1881), it is apparent that Wharton did not visualize a narrowly prescribed business curriculum but one in which instruction would be based "upon the broad principles deduced from all human knowledge; and ground in science, as well as in art, pupils . . . are thereby fitted both to practice what they have learned and to become themselves teachers and discoverers."

Certainly there was nothing in Wharton's rather eloquent statement-of-aims to suggest any necessary dichotomy between the goals of a business education and those of a liberal arts program. To some, however, it appeared that in the nature of academic reality, such a dichotomy was unpleasantly inevitable—an issue which was to be debated for many decades. Although we are getting ahead of our story, it is interesting to note that at the present time many educators and business executives are coming to the view that there is in fact no necessary dichotomy between liberal art offerings and business courses, and that the ultimate educational goals, in both instances, are quite similar. In this, of course, many of the original sentiments of Joseph Wharton are being echoed. At any rate, it is most unlikely that the latter had any idea of the academic controversy that would arise from the inception of collegiate business training; indeed, it is doubtful whether Wharton or anyone else could even have foreseen the huge numbers of business schools which were to follow the institution that bore his name. Reporting for the period 1900–1925, Marshall states:

> The new century thus began with collegiate education for business announced at seven institutions. The next decade saw ten more institutions added to the list; the next five years, twenty-three; and during the next nine years such a veritable craze for business education swept the country that one hundred and forty-three more were added; so that at the opening of the year 1925 one hundred and eighty-three (probably more) American colleges had "departments" or "schools" or "courses" or "divisions" or some other formally organized unit of instruction under the name of "business" or "com-

merce" or "business administration" or some other appropriate title.[2]

Following 1925, collegiate schools of business increased at an even faster tempo. Latest figures from the United States Office of Education indicate that of 1,393 institutions conferring undergraduate degrees in 1960, no less than 860 included "business and commerce" as a field of study![3] On the basis of official figures it can be seen that at the present time a substantial majority of American colleges are including business education as a regular part of their academic programs.

Another indication of the growth of collegiate business education can be seen from comparative figures based on male undergraduate degrees conferred. For the earlier period Bossard and Dewhurst compiled figures derived from the United States Bureau of Education, as follows:[4]

Male Undergraduate Degrees in Commerce

Year	Number
1914–15	615
1915–16	789
1917–18	610
1919–20	1,397
1921–22	3,205
1923–24	4,573
1925–26	4,972
1927–28	5,474

It can be seen that, in the 1927–1928 academic year, there were 5,474 undergraduate degrees in commerce granted. Latest statistics published by the United States Office of Education reveal that in 1960 the comparable figure was 47,629![5] An additional 6,816 degrees were granted in economics. As a matter of fact, the above data contain more than meets the eye: In 1927–28 there were 5,474 commerce degrees as compared to 27,263 arts and science degrees.

[2] Leon C. Marshall, "Schools of Commerce," *in* R. A. Kent (Ed.), *Higher Education in America* (Boston: Ginn and Co., 1930), pp. 78-79.
[3] U. S. Office of Education, *Earned Degrees Conferred by Higher Educational Institutions, 1959-1960*, Circular No. 687 (1962), Table 13, p. 21.
[4] James Bossard and J. Frederick Dewhurst, *University Education for Business* (Philadelphia: University of Pennsylvania Press, 1935), p. 256.
[5] U. S. Office of Education, *op. cit.,* Table 15, p. 35.

United States Office of Education figures for 1960 do not include a separate listing for the arts and science category; however, the 47,629 degrees conferred in business and commerce, plus the 6,816 granted in economics, *exceed the collective number of degrees granted* in the biological sciences, the physical sciences, English and journalism, foreign language and literature, philosophy, geography, sociology, history and anthropology.[6] Of all the fields of male undergraduate study enumerated by the United States Office of Education, the business and commerce area is by far the biggest single field, even surpassing in numbers the traditionally large areas of education and engineering.

With regard to *total enrollment* of business students, Hughes has presented an eye-catching estimate of things to come:

> Starting from a few thousand students in 1910, collegiate education in business had grown to more than 350,000 students by 1955. In fact, one of the most pressing problems in higher education today is how to meet the rising tide of students during the next decade. . . . In 1900, only about 4 per cent of the age-eligible population attended college. Since 1950, the college attendance ratio has approached 30 per cent. These enrollment growths are having a marked effect on collegiate schools of business. By 1970, it is estimated that over 600,000 young men and women will be pursuing programs in the collegiate schools of business.[7]

Insofar as numbers are concerned, it does not appear that our society will lack for businessmen!

It should be pointed out, also, that as the number of business schools increased, and as the enrollment in these schools skyrocketed, business schools themselves proliferated into an almost endless variety of offerings. Whether business courses proliferated in response to mushrooming enrollment, or whether the enrollment followed the increase in course offerings is not clear. It seems likely that, numerically, students and courses were mutually supplementary. In any event, the business offerings grew and grew.

The pioneer schools centered their business offerings largely

[6] *Ibid.*, derived from Table 15, pp. 35-38.

[7] Eugene Hughes, "The Need for Discovering the Fundamental Bases of Higher Education for Business," *American Business Education Association Yearbook*, Vol. 14 (1957), pp. 57-58.

around accounting, mercantile law, and certain aspects of applied economics. Slowly at first, but at an increasing rate, business and commercial activities were conceived in functional terms such as corporation finance, production, management, and marketing. After World War II, basic courses in the functional fields came to be followed by more specialized, "advanced" courses in these same fields. Basic courses in marketing, for instance, often led to courses in advertising and sales promotion; a principles course in business management might lead to specialized courses in personnel and labor relations, et cetera. Other functional areas were shown to have utilitarian value, and courses in real estate, insurance, transportation, and foreign trade soon dotted the curriculum. These, in turn, came to be followed by sequences of advanced, highly specialized courses.

On the basis of their 1930 survey Bossard and Dewhurst reported that:

> The business studies taught in present day curricula of collegiate schools of business include accounting, banking and finance, business law, marketing, advertising, selling, merchandising, foreign trade and foreign service, insurance, business organization and management, labor and personnel, public utilities, real estate, statistics and business cycles, and transportation and traffic. . . . Numerous courses of instruction and specialized curricula are offered in each of the fields referred to above. These subjects have developed, for the most part, without regard each to the other, or the central project of the training of students for business. The result has been a multitude of courses, with considerable duplication of material and very little coordination. What the business schools have accomplished has been the development of certain phases of business much more than a unified program of business education.[8]

That the business courses had proliferated could not be denied, although the contention of Bossard and Dewhurst relative to course duplication and lack of program unification was, at the time, denied by some, affirmed by others. In the section of his report dealing with "Trends in Business Curricula," however, Bossard and Dewhurst stated that:

> Further specialization is being frowned upon, at least so far as undergraduate curricula and instruction are concerned . . . There

[8] Bossard and Dewhurst, *op. cit.,* pp. 458-460.

seems to be a trend towards fewer courses, or, at least to the very careful scrutiny of new courses. This is partly a matter of administrative economy, and partly a matter of educational policy. There is a widespread belief that the proliferation of courses has run riot.[9]

In this, time proved Bossard and Dewhurst wrong, for it wasn't long before such courses as fire insurance, hotel management, airline management, motion picture operations, et cetera, were being offered in at least some business schools. Writing in 1957, Hamilton commented on the large number of courses currently available in collegiate schools of business; e.g., "New York University School of Commerce, 361; University of Illinois, 173; University of Denver, 292; State College of Washington, 134. These are representative enough to illustrate the tremendous growth in number of subjects classified and/or administered in business subjects."[10] The same writer states that:

Offerings in the various fields or departments are often very elaborate and specialized. The number of undergraduate courses and credits in various subjects in the following schools illustrates how finely subdivided the offerings have become:

Michigan State College has 23 courses with 70 quarter hours of credit in accounting.

New York University College of Commerce, Accounts, and Finance has 20 courses with 57 semester hours of credit in accounting. In the Department of Management and Industrial Relations, one finds 26 courses with 77 semester hours of credit.

The University of Texas lists 21 courses with 53 credits in marketing; 14 courses and 45 credits in personnel and industrial relations; and 9 courses and 27 hours in transportation.

Syracuse University offers 14 courses with 48 credits in marketing; 14 courses and 45 credits in personnel and industrial relations; and 9 courses and 27 hours in transportation.

At Southwestern Louisiana Institute, a smaller and newly established College of Commerce offers 12 courses and 50 semester hours in accounting.

That this expansion and subdivision of subject matter has gone unquestioned and without challenge is certainly not true. It has been

[9] *Ibid.*, p. 476.
[10] Herbert A. Hamilton, "The Present Status of Higher Education for Business," *American Business Education Association Yearbook*, Vol. 14 (1957), p. 43.

seriously challenged by educators and by the results and follow-up studies of graduates.[11]

It is true that the proliferation of courses has been in evidence in the non-business areas, including the liberal arts; in fact, one could argue that the expansion of courses in any area merely reflects a growing body of substantive knowledge, and that this is all to the good. But it can also be argued that academic over-specialization of any kind tends to thwart the very purpose of higher learning. Some of the pros and cons of this issue will be explored in the following pages.

[11] *Ibid.*, p. 44.

Chapter 3

THE ROLE OF LIBERAL ARTS PRIOR TO
WORLD WAR II

DIFFERENCES BETWEEN BUSINESS EDUCATION AND OTHER
AREAS OF SPECIALIZATION

IN MANY WAYS THE HISTORY OF HIGHER EDUCATION IS THE HISTORY
of specialized education. Starting with a classics-oriented liberal arts
program, collegiate education has grown in the direction of specialized training in medicine, law, engineering, et cetera. And whereas
college was formerly deemed to be a privilege reserved for the well-
to-do, over the years democratic sentiment has favored a policy of
"education for the many." Collegiate business training differed from
other specialized areas in a number of ways: For one thing, as has
been mentioned, it was one of the last arrivals on the specialized-
education scene. For another, business education was more firmly
rooted in the liberal arts tradition than were areas like law, engineering, medicine, dentistry, and architecture. And as Bossard and Dewhurst pointed out, "Curricula, like men, elephants, and ant eaters,
are what they are because of their ancestry. Business curricula are
descendants of that imperious dowager of academic life—the liberal
arts college . . . and perhaps no factor has been so persistently important in shaping the curricula of the collegiate schools of business,
as well as in other phases of their development."[1]

Originally, collegiate business education was centered in the lib-

[1] James Bossard and J. Frederick Dewhurst, *University Education for Business*
(Philadelphia: University of Pennsylvania Press, 1935), pp. 317-318.

32

eral arts college, with the latter providing both the physical facilities and the teaching personnel. From all reports, the initial endeavors could hardly be called successful. By and large, liberal arts teachers had little experience—and even less interest—in the business areas. It might be expected, in this early period, that the economics department would be the logical instrument with which to attempt an integration of business and liberal arts, but such was not the case. From the very beginning, economics departments were prone to take a somewhat jaundiced view toward the business newcomers, a view which is still somewhat in evidence.[2] Even at the present time, economics departments are divided in their affiliation, some being located in the school of business, others in the liberal arts college.[3] At any rate, from the view of liberal arts integration, the launching of the collegiate business school took place in turbulent waters. Commenting on the early Wharton School experience, Edmund James wrote:

> There were no models which we could follow. There was no experience from which we could profit. The funds themselves were inadequate for the purpose in hand. The other departments in the University and most of the other members of the faculty were bitterly opposed to the whole project. And even if they did not actually interfere to prevent the progress of the work, they stood with watchful, jealous eyes to see that no concession of any sort should be made to these new subjects which, in their opinion, might in any way lower the level of scholarship as the ideal had been accepted by the upholders of the traditional courses.[4]

[2] For a comprehensive discussion of the role of economics in education, see Walter J. Matherly, "The Relationship of the School of Business to the College of Liberal Arts," *American Association of Collegiate Schools of Business, Proceedings of the 19th Annual Meeting* (March 1937), pp. 5-17; and Paul Olson, "The Professional Economist and Economic Education," *Collegiate News and Views*, Vol. 11 (March 1958), pp. 1-6.

[3] Based on a questionnaire survey, Howard Cutler found that in the larger universities, economics departments tended to be located in the colleges of liberal arts, while in the "smaller" institutions (enrollment less than 15,000) the economics departments were more likely to be found in the schools of business: "Organization of Collegiate Schools of Business," *Collegiate News and Views*, Vol. 7 (October 1953), pp. 1-8.

[4] Cf. Edmund James, "Origin and Progress of Business Education in the United States," address at a University of Illinois conference, 1913, quoted in Benjamin Haynes and Harry Jackson, *A History of Business Education in the United States* (Cincinnati, Ohio: South-Western Publishing Co., 1935), p. 89.

Another difference between business education and other emergent specialties like medicine and law was the fact that business was not originally conceived as professional training. From the very beginning, therefore, business educators were put in the unenviable position of providing specialized training as thorough as that offered in medicine and law, and at the same time of providing a general education as extensive as that offered in the liberal arts college. This double-exposure predicament was, and in many ways still is, the crux of the argument insofar as business education is concerned.

The above dilemma was solved, in this earlier period, by structuring business education in terms of the student's first job. Along with a liberal arts education, the student was expected to acquire such business skills as would be necessary to acquire a functional position in the business world. It should be noted that the business school catalogues did not state the matter in such mundane terms; in fact, according to the objectives outlined in the catalogues, the primary function of business education was often held to be that of training for business "leadership." R. A. Stevenson is of the opinion that these early catalogue statements on leadership were made for the purpose of refuting the "vocational" charges made by the more established sections of the academic community.[5] It is apparent, however, catalogue claims to the contrary, that between World War I and World War II business education was basically of a specialized, functional nature.

In many ways the business schools were supplying what industry wanted, and in retrospect this is hardly surprising. In the 1920's business was humming, the stock market was surging, and making money was considered by some to be a veritable national pastime. Social codes and moral values were undergoing fairly drastic changes. In such an atmosphere it is little wonder that so-called materialistic values should make themselves felt in the educational world, and that large numbers of parents should wish to send their sons to college to learn to "be something."

[5] Russell A. Stevenson, "The Proposed Survey of Business Education," *American Association of Collegiate Schools of Business, Proceedings of the 21st Annual Meeting* (April 1939), pp. 8-26.

REACTIONS OF LIBERAL ARTS ADVOCATES

The specialistic trend in business education was looked upon with various degrees of alarm by the advocates of generalized, liberal arts instruction. As long ago as 1918 Thorstein Veblen penned the following vitriolic criticism of business education:

> The primacy among pragmatic interests has passed from religion to business, and the school of commerce is the exponent of this primacy. It is the perfect flower of the secularization of the universities.[6]
> The professional knowledge and skill of physicians, surgeons, dentists, pharmacists, agriculturists, engineers of all kinds, perhaps even of journalists, is of some use to the community at large, at the same time that it may be profitable to the bearers of it . . . . But such is not the case with the training designed to give proficiency in business. No gain comes to the community at large from increasing the business proficiency of any number of its young men. There are already much too many of these businessmen, much too astute and proficient in their calling, for the common good. A higher average business efficiency simply raises activity and avidity in business to a higher average pitch and fervour, with very little other material result than a redistribution of ownership; since business is occupied with the competitive acquisition of wealth, not with its production . . . . The work of the College of Commerce, accordingly, is a peculiarly futile line of endeavor for any public institution, in that it serves neither the intellectual advancement nor the material welfare of the community."[7]

The sentiments in the above quotation are extreme, of course, but other writers, even though more temperate in their statements, nevertheless took a dim view of the path of business education. Writing in the *North American Review* in 1930, L. J. Natiens bemoaned the drift toward specialized commercial training. Natiens felt that a large percentage of American youth were choosing the field of business education, and that unless the latter were liberally oriented, both the student and society would ultimately suffer: "Culture cannot be

[6] Thorstein Veblen, *The Higher Learning in America* (New York: B. W. Huebsch, 1918), p. 205.
[7] *Ibid.*, pp. 208-209.

grafted upon a business man, or upon a business community, as a limb can be grafted upon a tree."[8]

A few years later Bossard and Dewhurst wrote:

> Successful business management, it is true, demands adequate technical knowledge of business practice and procedure, but it is by no means certain that the undergraduate business school is the proper place for the acquisition of such knowledge. Certainly there is a growing tendency on the part of employers of college labor to deplore the further development of specialized "practical" courses in the undergraduate curriculum. There is general agreement that a mere knowledge of business facts and principles gained at second hand is of far less importance in preparing the student for a business career than the development of his capacity for applying imagination and intelligence in attacking and solving concrete problems.[9]

Of special interest in the above quotation is the statement that employers tended to look with disfavor on the further development of "practical" courses, for in the same period (1931) Lyon, on the basis of questioning business leaders, concluded that they did indeed want generalists rather than specialists. A few of the statements were anti-liberal arts: "I do not employ college men in my banking office . . . . The college man is not willing to begin at the bottom . . . . His thoughts are not with his business, but with his books, literature, philosophy, Latin . . . ." The large majority of responses, however, indicated that business employers wanted men with "broad vision," with a grasp of "cultural dynamics," an appreciation of "community responsibility" etc.[10]

A few liberal arts educators, in this earlier period, saw some genuine value in business education. Henry W. Stuart, Professor of Philosophy at Stanford University, while criticizing some aspects of "vocational" education, wrote: "Even if a 'vocationally centered' education is thus deficient, so also is a purely liberal education, through its exclusion of vocational elements. Liberal education is not really adequate and thorough on its own ground and in its own way if it

[8]L. J. Natiens, "Business Before Culture," *North American Review,* Vol. 229 (June 1930), p. 711.

[9]Bossard and Dewhurst, *op. cit.,* pp. 565-566.

[10]S. Leverett Lyon, *Education for Business* (Chicago: University of Chicago Press, 1931), p. 63.

fails to recognize along with those other interests and institutions which it makes a point of acknowledging. In fact the vocational interest affords a peculiarly favorable opening for the presentation of the liberal subjects."[11]

Statements like Stuart's, however, were clearly in the minority. Most liberal arts people were skeptical of the educational value of the so-called vocational business training, and took little pains to hide their feelings. And on the other side of the unfortunate—but very real—fence, business educators were just as outspoken in their defense of business education.

VIEWS OF BUSINESS EDUCATORS

In the twenties, thirties, and early forties, business educators not only defended the role of their discipline but raised serious questions regarding the value of traditional liberal arts training. A number of men in the functional business fields felt that generalized liberal arts education had simply not proved itself, and that the decline in this type of training was, Q.E.D., inevitable. Other business educators were of the opinion that the liberal arts subjects were just as specialized and "vocational" as were the business subjects. In 1941, R. A. Stevenson, Dean of the University of Minnesota Business School, observed that, whereas prior to World War I liberal arts colleges had been non-vocational in nature, they had become increasingly oriented toward such "practical" majors as teaching, commercial art, government service, social work, and journalism. It was Stevenson's belief that if this vocational emphasis had occurred *prior* to World War I, when business education was coming into its own, the business schools would have remained within the liberal arts fold.[12]

Some business educators took the view that the values of a liberal arts education, while significant, were capable of being realized only through superior teachers, and that too much of what had passed for

[11] Henry W. Stuart, *Liberal and Vocational Studies in the College* (Stanford, Calif.: Stanford University Press, 1918), pp. 3-4.

[12] Russell A. Stevenson, "The Relationship Between a College of Commerce and a Liberal Arts Division," *American Association of Collegiate Schools of Business, Proceedings of the 23rd Annual Meeting* (May 1941), pp. 65-68.

humanistic education was in reality a combination of unrelated facts and rote learning. Writing on a somewhat similar historical theme, the Wharton Survey Advisory Committee (of which the present writers were members) commented as follows:

> The purpose of such (liberal arts) courses is to provide the student with a fuller awareness of humanistic, cultural, and literary values, and to promote a keener understanding and appreciation of man and his environment. Through such an orientation it is believed that students will be able to assume responsible citizenship and, in a very real sense, to lead fuller and richer lives. But however admirable the purpose, it is palpably not true that these potential benefits *inhere* in a course just because it is labelled liberal arts. The values and benefits of liberal arts offerings are usually implicit and subtle rather than explicit and concrete. A generation or so ago liberal arts education went into a decline, and was replaced in part by business, professional, and other more "practical" forms of education. It was not utilitarian education alone which drove out the liberal arts but bad liberal arts.[13]

There is apparently much truth in the foregoing statement, although it could also be argued that with the temper of the times being what they were, the best liberal arts courses in the world couldn't have stopped the tide of business education. Be that as it may, however, the point is that business educators in the twenties and thirties did not rely solely on defensive arguments.

It should be mentioned that even in this earlier period, there was some internal sentiment in favor of liberalizing the business curriculum. Around 1920 Dean Donham of Harvard began to espouse the cause of a broad, liberal business education program, and later at the same school the work of Elton Mayo in industrial sociology helped to lay the groundwork for what was later to be called the "human relations" approach to industrial management.[14] The University of Pennsylvania's Wharton School came to include certain of the social science departments as an integral part of the school's organizational structure. Also, in 1916, the American Association of Collegiate

[13] Wharton Survey Advisory Committee, *A Program for the Wharton School,* Mimeographed report (Philadelphia: University of Pennsylvania, 1957), p. 38.

[14] See Richard Hofstadter and C. DeWitt Hardy, *The Development and Scope of Higher Education in the United States* (New York: Columbia University Press, 1952), pp. 92-93, and Keith Davis, "Human Relations as a Basis," *American Business Education Association Yearbook,* Vol. 14 (1957), pp. 136-149.

Schools of Business (A.A.C.S.B.) was formed, and in 1924 a Standards Committee of the Association recommended that one of the membership requirements be that "at least forty per cent of the total hours required for the bachelor's degree must be taken in subjects other than business and economics."[15] This recommendation was adopted in 1925 and has been in force ever since.[16]

In the period of which we are writing, however, steps toward liberalizing the business curriculum were overshadowed by the trend toward course-proliferation in the functional areas. Liberal arts education, in the view of many business educators, was simply tolerated. Thus in a speech delivered before the annual meeting of the American Association of Collegiate Schools of Business in 1935, Paul Nystrom, professor of marketing at an Ivy League university could state that:

> The suggestions so far made apply to collegiate schools of business whose purpose is the training for business. The so-called regular or conventional college training may be quite a different matter. I do not question the value of the conventional college course. Its usefulness of keeping young people for a period of four years out of the market place for employment may be socially desirable. Such college courses may contribute many delightful as well as useful social graces including smatterings of information concerning the sciences, history, literature, the languages and other arts. All of this provides an interesting finish for those who complete their courses satisfactorily. How much of this turns out to be of value as preparation for participation in the major currents of present day life is a question that need not be discussed here. Our responsibility as teachers and administrators in collegiate schools of business is to make sure that what we offer actually fits the needs of our students who are going into business. Our work is clearly cut out for us.[17]

And as late as 1944 a prominent business educator and president of a leading midwestern university, in an address before an education and industry conference, could report that:

[15] *Constitution and Standards for Membership* (pamphlet), (St. Louis, Mo.: American Association of Collegiate Schools of Business, 1962), p. 3.

[16] *Ibid.*

[17] Paul H. Nystrom, "College Training and the New Deal," *American Association of Collegiate Schools of Business, Proceedings of the 17th Annual Meeting* (April 1935), pp. 20-27.

Education wants industry to define, so far as possible, the abilities, capacities, knowledges, skills, and attitudes required for various kinds of employment. Education wants business and industry to provide for it a chart which can be followed in its training program. Education recognizes that possession of a Bachelor's or a Master's degree may not be an indication of education as desired by industry, and, moreover, that all too often the first task of business has been to "uneducate" the newly employed young graduate. Therefore, if business and industry will tell education through job analyses what it desires that they *know,* education on the secondary and higher levels can proceed much more intelligently to construct training programs that will meet actual needs.[18]

HISTORICAL SUMMARY

In brief, the period between the two World Wars saw a rapid rise in the number of business schools, the number of business offerings, and the number of students majoring in the functional business areas. Insofar as business education policy was concerned the emphasis in most schools was on a practical preparation for a specific job in industry and commerce. Lip service was often paid to the idea of training for managerial "leadership," but the proliferation and specialization of functional business courses confuted any such claim. As a matter of fact, more than one business educator was willing to go on record as saying, in effect, "if industry tells us what it wants in the way of skills and special training, we will do our best to meet the need."

Liberal arts educators, as a group, were somewhat aghast at what they felt was a turn toward vocational education, and showed no hesitancy in voicing their opinions. On their part, business educators were just as quick to point the "education for what?" finger at the liberal arts advocates. But whatever the merits of the respective arguments, the temper of the times was on the side of the business practitioners, and insofar as the end result was concerned, the period between the wars must in retrospect be looked upon more or less as

[18] Reported in A. L. Prickett and H. V. Olsen, *The Collegiate Schools of Business in American Education, Third Annual Delta Pi Epsilon Lecture,* December 28, 1944 (Cincinnati, Ohio: South-Western Publishing Co., 1944), pp. 20-21.

a hiatus in the continuum of liberal educational policy.

It should be noted that a few liberal arts advocates professed to see some value in business education programs, and that some business educators were critical of the "vocational" type of training provided in many business schools. In this connection, the A.A.C.S.B.'s "40 per cent liberal arts" requirement was considered by many to be a step in the right direction. In general, though, insofar as business education was concerned, the rejuvenation of the liberal arts program and the protest against the so-called vocational type of business program were events which were not to manifest themselves until the post-World War II period.

Chapter 4

THE POST-WORLD WAR II PERIOD—
A CHANGE IN CLIMATE

IT CAN PROBABLY BE SAID OF ALL SOCIAL INSTITUTIONS THAT change-of-action is preceded by change-of-thinking. In the case at hand, collegiate schools of business are undergoing a change-of-thinking, and in many cases action programs have already crystallized. In both instances the change relates both indirectly and directly to a felt need for greater emphasis on liberal arts content. The reasons for this liberal arts interest can perhaps only be conjectured, but the following factors appear to be relevant:

(*a*) After World War II it became clear that international problems would be a major concern for many decades, and that these problems would be capable of solution only by public officials with the broadest range of knowledge and breadth of vision.

(*b*) The American people were having more and more leisure time at their command, with a consequent problem of how to spend it.

(*c*) As leisure increased, general plane-of-living also rose, with the result that there was more opportunity for the pursuit of cultural and aesthetic rewards. Not that most people actually took advantage of this opportunity—but it would seem in this respect that persons most likely to reap the rewards were those whose education had included substantive offerings in history, literature, philosophy, social science, and the fine arts.

(*d*) There was a growing feeling that the business leader of tomorrow would have to be a man with sufficient breadth of knowledge to relate specific business problems to the more general social, political, and civic problems of which industry was finding itself an integral part.

(*e*) Finally, there was a feeling on the part of certain business educators that the highly specialized business courses had simply not proved themselves.

Maynard Peck, head of the economics department at Sterling College, wrote that these courses had not only failed to prove themselves but that the graduates "were poorly prepared to meet the real-life problems as encountered in the business world itself . . . They could not meet the public nor could they make the necessary social adjustments needed for success in the business community."[1] The same author goes on to say that "The business world is finding that men who have graduated from a liberal arts college are prominent among those who are out in front in the battle to raise the standards of the business world. Because of these men, progress is being made toward the goal of higher business ethics and a keener sense of social responsibility in modern business and industry."[2] (And while Peck believes strongly in business education, he believes the latter should be a functional aspect of liberal arts training.)

Some indirect empirical support for Peck's views is found in the (1952) best-selling *They Went to College,* by Ernest Havemann and Patricia West. In Chapter Twelve, the authors attempt to pin down "the long argument which has raged over specific versus general education . . .: Who is the more successful—the A.B. or the specialist?" Since the Havemann-West study was based on a random sample of 9,064 college graduate respondents, the results of their questionnaire were most significant. Insofar as actual salaries are concerned, the specialist—including the business major—comes out clearly ahead of the education, humanities, and social science majors.[3] However, good statistical evidence indicates that whereas the generalist makes less money, he apparently makes a better citizen than does his

---

[1] Maynard Peck, "Business Education in the Liberal Arts College," *Association of American Colleges Bulletin,* Vol. 41 (May 1955), p. 299.

[2] *Ibid.*

[3] Ernest Havemann and Patricia West, *They Went to College* (New York: Harcourt, Brace, and Co., 1952), p. 149.

specialized brother: "It is quite clear that the generally educated graduates are the most active and interested citizens of their communities and their nation. They are much less likely to be 'narrow specialists' in their private lives. They play a more active and varied role in society, and perhaps a more useful and rewarding as well."[4] Other findings: about one-third of the business majors were dissatisfied with their choice of a major, but this same figure also applied to those majoring in history, literature, languages, and social sciences; in fact, when the figures are broken down it developed that the generalist who "specialized in nothing" was the most dissatisfied of all. Havemann and West conclude by saying: "Perhaps the great question which all statistics and letters from our survey pose, on the matter we are considering in this chapter, is just this: In our tremendously complicated modern world, and for a student who must both learn to earn a living and learn to live with his conscience, can either the general or the special education be enough by itself?"[5]

STATEMENTS BY BUSINESS EDUCATORS

Whatever the reasons for liberal arts "revival," the periodical literature of the last decade or so is filled with statements by business educators citing the need for increased emphasis on education oriented within a liberal, humanistic framework. The rationale, or reasoning, behind the call for liberal arts takes a number of forms. Some business educators feel that business courses themselves, potentially at least, contain much in the way of liberal arts content. Michael McPhelin, former Dean of the Fordham University School of Business, referring to the role of business education, states:

> Not only can it be taught liberally but it is clamoring to be taught liberally. It has more to teach . . . than much of Horace and Sappho, Thackeray and Faulkner . . . Business is worthy of a close examination. It is a work of man, an intricate structure of important, day-to-day, social relations. If society be worthy of study, why not the social edifice which is the world of business? . . . Business as well as litera-

[4] *Ibid.*, p. 150.
[5] *Ibid.*, p. 156.

ture contains materials helpful in teaching us to know man and his world.[6]

Some business educators are of the opinion that insofar as objectives are concerned it is not feasible to try to separate business education and general education. As Carl W. Hansen puts it:

> There can be no real separation of general education and professional education, since the basic/foundation of all professional education *is* general education. A professional man is a citizen with special training and a special job to do. He cannot disassociate himself from the society in which he labors. A functional program of general education seeks to provide the social viewpoint which the professional man needs and which in some professions he has not obtained in the pre-war professional curricula. It is already apparent that some professional schools are aware of this need and are modifying their programs so as to include greater cultural emphasis within their curricula.[7]

Courtney Brown, Dean of the Columbia University Graduate School of Business, believes that advanced programs in business can be broad and can be "taught in the great liberal tradition." He cites four developments: (1) A greater use of mathematical tools; (2) The introduction into the business curriculum of behavorial sciences; (3) A reclassification of business subjects; and (4) A rebirth of interest in the humanities. In the latter connection, he states:

> This may be the most exciting challenge of all in the years ahead, for it seems to imply a greater awareness of the quasi-political status in which the business manager now finds himself. It suggests that the great minds of yesterday, working with the problems of politics and ethics in a different setting, have much to offer for an understanding of the contemporary position of business and its opportunities in society.[8]

Speaking of the business courses at his own college, Roger S. Hamilton, Dean of the Northeastern University College of Business Administration, reports:

[6] Rev. Michael McPhelin, "The Humanities in Education for Business," *Collegiate News and Views,* Vol. 8 (October 1954), pp. 1-6.

[7] Carl W. Hansen, "Curriculum Practices on the College and University Level," *American Business Education Association Yearbook,* Vol. 5 (1947), p. 215.

[8] Courtney Brown, "Business in Cap and Gown," *Saturday Review,* Vol. 40 (January 19, 1957), p. 18.

We try to develop an historical perspective, and awareness of underlying principles and precepts . . . and *lastly* we try to develop the student's vocational interest and aptitude.[9]

A number of business educators advocate increased emphasis on liberal arts, pointing out, among other things, that the demands of today's society are such that business leaders must be men of broad gauge perspective and vision. Morris E. Hurley, Dean of the College of Business Administration, Syracuse University, in writing along these lines, states that:

The purposes of liberal arts training for business students do not differ significantly from the purposes of such training for students of any other profession or trade. Yet, far more is involved in general or liberal arts training for business students than merely the personal enrichment of the business student's life. Business administrators are key men in modern industrial society. Frequently, they are called upon to exercise generalized leadership with respect to their fellow men as well as to contribute the fruits of their functional competence to the general welfare. Business leaders who can approach modern problems with breadth and perspective are needed at local, state, national, and international levels. The exercise of inspired and responsible leadership calls for an understanding of human aspirations and values, plus a sense of participation in the triumphs and tragedies of one's fellow men . . . The approaches to general or liberal arts education that are advocated by many business administration curriculum-builders are tied in closely . . . with the endeavor to achieve understanding of inter-relationships among the basic forces that exist in the world about us.[10]

A growing number of business educators believe that business should become a profession, following the patterns set by medicine and law, and that professionalized business training should have as a prerequisite an undergraduate degree in the arts and sciences. Certain business schools have already adopted a program of this kind. Joseph F. Bradley, Professor of Finance at Pennsylvania State College of Business Administration, advocates such a policy and

[9] Roger S. Hamilton, "Business Administration Courses Adjusted to Community Needs," *American Business Education*, Vol. 7 (May 1951), p. 283. (Italics added.)

[10] Morris E. Hurley, "Liberal Arts as a Basis," *American Business Education Association Yearbook*, Vol. 14 (1957), pp. 68-69.

offers the following requirements for professionalization: "(1) The members who engage in the activity must believe that mankind has the ability to improve himself indefinitely. (2) The members who engage in the activity must believe that ethical standards are of prime importance. (3) The activity must consist of the application of an advanced body of knowledge which can be acquired only by a long period of training in a university . . . . (4) The public must believe that its interests are served best by state licensure or by some other equivalent method of limiting entrants into the activity. (5) The members who engage in the activity must be banded together into a strong professional organization."[11] The same writer goes on to say that:

> Knowledge that is useful for all citizens consists of an understanding of the humanities, the social sciences, and the sciences—both physical and biological . . . . In all these fields, the professional person is expected to have done serious study; i.e., to have read some of the works of the great thinkers, to have integrated the contributions of a number of the great thinkers into a personal philosophy of life, and to have generated an inquiring state of mind that will last a lifetime . . . . A plan that will aid in the professionalization of business is to require the individual aspirants to have a Bachelor of Arts Degree, a Master of Business Administration Degree, and a period of service as an apprentice . . . at least one business activity—that of accounting—has already reached professional status. There are a number of fields of business which are just a step away from professional status.[12]

Robinson, in a recent (1962) statement in the *Journal of Higher Education,* spells out some of the reasons for a shift of emphasis to the sphere of graduate business education: "The specific reasons for the shift of business education to the graduate level are now familiar. As universities seek to enlarge the analytical core of professional education for business, they place greater demands on the student, and must draw on a richer background than that usually possessed by a Freshman or even a Junior. Analytically oriented programs in business are based to a great extent on the concepts and methods of of other disciplines—and are, in effect, dealing with advanced work

---

[11] Joseph F. Bradley, "The Emergence of Business as a Profession," *Collegiate News and Views,* Vol. 11 (March 1958), p. 11.

[12] *Ibid.,* pp. 14-15.

in those disciplines. Thus such business schools are virtually forced to work with graduate students, for the same reasons that graduate education in these disciplines is demanded."[13]

It should be mentioned, parenthetically, that a few collegiate schools of business have converted; i.e., they have become solely graduate centers, with programs leading to the M.B.A. or Ph.D. In a realistic sense, however, one wonders whether the trend toward graduate business "conversion" has about run its course. As Gordon and Howell put it: "There is still uncertainty as to how much effort should be put into expanding graduate training at the expense of the undergraduate program. The exclusively graduate schools have reached one answer, but one that most business schools are not prepared to accept and which is beyond the reach of most departments (as distinct from schools) of business."[14]

STATEMENTS BY BUSINESS LEADERS

The post-war call by business educators for more emphasis on liberal arts education was repeated, and in many cases, amplified by the public statements of a variety of business leaders. As a matter of fact, on the basis of speeches, public statements, and press releases, it would seem that business executives were in a rush to board the liberal arts bandwagon. Statements quoted in the *Wall Street Journal, Business Week, Fortune,* etc., gave ample proof that the men in charge of the nation's business foresaw a bull market in the liberal arts.

Gilbert W. Chapman, President of Yale and Towne Manufacturing Company, reports that technical specialty "is in itself not sufficient qualification for top-executive responsibility," and calls for "more general education for our specialists," and "a new, strong emphasis on the liberal arts as a preparation for careers in executive

[13] Marshall A. Robinson, "The Academic Content of Business Education," *Journal of Higher Education,* Vol. 33, No. 3 (March 1962), p. 133.

[14] Robert A. Gordon and James E. Howell, *Higher Education for Business* (New York: Columbia University Press, 1959), p. 248.

management."[15] Examples of other statements are reported below.

Abram Collier, Vice President of John Hancock Life Insurance Company:

> The Chinese wall between business and the home, the community, the school, and the church has long since been stormed. Business is all people, places, and things; it is physics, economics, political science, sociology, psychology, philosophy, ethics, and aesthetics.[16]

Irving Olds, Chairman of the Board of United States Steel Corporation:

> The most difficult problems which American enterprise faces today are neither scientific nor technical, but lie chiefly in the realm of what is embraced in a liberal arts education.[17]

Ralph M. Besse, Vice President of Cleveland Electric Illuminating Company:

> Liberal arts will be essential to give the prospective business leader some comprehension of man's relations to man—his psychology, his origins, his understanding, his motivation.[18]

Albert L. Nickerson, Vice President and Director of Foreign Trade of Socony-Vacuum Oil Company:

> Our business system, indeed our whole scheme of contemporary American Life, requires the education of young men and women of moral stamina who can think and who can discriminate among values. This implies the necessity for the continued extension of a sound liberal education to every American boy and girl with the capacity to assimilate it.[19]

Clarence B. Randall, retired Chairman of the Board of Inland Steel Company:

[15] Quoted in W. W. Brickman, "Liberal Education and Industrial Leadership," *School and Society*, Vol. 85 (September 14, 1957), p. 253.

[16] From Weldon Taylor, "Are Business Schools Meeting the Challenge?" *Collegiate News and Views*, Vol. 10 (October 1956), p. 2.

[17] *Ibid.*

[18] Ralph M. Besse, "The Vision of the Future," *Vital Speeches*, Vol. 23, No. 18 (July 1957), p. 554.

[19] Albert L. Nickerson, "Climbing the Managerial Ladder," *Saturday Review*, Vol. 36 (November 21, 1953), p. 39.

For the perpetuation of management in corporate life we require men trained in the creative and imaginative qualities that come from a general education. We want, first of all, a man who has demonstrated that he can master any subject. And above all, we require a man who has the intellectual courage to tackle something for which he was not trained. A business leader must be able to walk with confidence on unfamiliar ground.[20]

Robert D. Calkins, Vice President and Director of the General Education Board, makes the following interesting comments, apropos of the views of business leaders:[21] "It has been my experience in talking with businessmen about college preparation for business, that the higher up you go the greater will be the emphasis placed upon a broad education. The top officials stress broad rather than specialized preparation. The executives lower down do not. The latter stress specialized skills." When company presidents are asked about the kind of men they are looking for, Calkins states that the latter reply, "We want men, first of all, who are broadly trained, who have good minds and good character and good personalities. We'll teach them the details of this business after we get them here on the job."

STATEMENTS BY LIBERAL ARTS PEOPLE

The views of liberal arts advocates—both academicians and non-academicians—in the postwar period are somewhat more difficult to gauge. All things considered, there seems to be less criticism directed against specialized education in general and against business programs specifically. On the contrary, the position is apparently being taken that both types of education have much in common, and that insofar as over-all goals are concerned, the aims of both business and liberal arts education are complementary and in many ways similar.

W. D. Patterson, associate publisher of the *Saturday Review,* editorializes that business education in the vocational sense is being

---

[20] Quoted in David A. Shepard, *Liberal Education in an Industrial Society,* Public Affairs Pamphlet No. 248 (New York: Public Affairs Committee, 1957) p. 16.

[21] Robert D. Calkins, "Liberal Arts in Business Training," *Association of American Colleges Bulletin,* Vol. 38 (May 1952), p. 330.

superseded by professional training "in which the subject is related in meaningful terms to the basic liberal tradition of learning." It is Patterson's feeling that what the business world wants is fundamentally a liberal arts man with professional training in business.[22]

Writing in *School and Society,* Lawrence C. Lockley states that "Essentially there need be little difference in the substantive content of courses in colleges of liberal arts and in schools of business . . . . Political science, statistics, history . . . sociology . . . these are the foundation of the sound business education. And they are equally appropriate to the college of liberal arts . . . . Just as the essential greatness of the humanities lies in the particular emphasis, so the essential greatness of business lies in the emphasis that is, or that should be, given in the schools of commerce . . . . As we near our objectives, we will find a closer kinship between the humanities and business education."[23]

OTHER EVIDENCE OF CLIMATIC CHANGE

We have quoted extensively from business educators, business executives, and liberal arts people, in order to show that at least at the verbal level most of the interested parties seem to feel that what is called for is a reorientation of existing business programs in terms of a more liberal, humanistic philosophy. In a similar vein, other signs of the times are unmistakingly appearing. For instance, in 1957 for the first time the widely distributed Public Affairs Pamphlet Series included a twenty-eight-page pamphlet on *Liberal Education in an Industrial Society.* Written by David A. Shepard, a member of the board of directors of Standard Oil of New Jersey and a trustee of the Massachusetts Institute of Technology, the pamphlet points up the value of liberal training in today's industrial world. Shepard states that:

Now, as never before, our industrial society is interested in the

[22] W. D. Patterson, "Business: Our Newest Profession," *Saturday Review,* Vol. 40 (January 19, 1957), p. 28.

[23] Lawrence C. Lockley, "Business Education and the Humanities," *School and Society,* Vol. 5 (December 29, 1951), pp. 418-420.

college student and in the place where he is spending his four years. It is alert to the contributions students trained in the humanities can make to our society as well as those trained in the practical sciences. It is ready to assure students that even their seemingly non-vocational training will stand them in good stead in the world of business . . . . [24]

Worthy of mention, also, is the fact that in the same year, 1957, the *American Business Education Association Yearbook* was devoted in its entirety to the subject of "Education for Business Beyond High School," with several sections being devoted to the role of liberal arts.[25]

Because of their wide circulation the *Public Affairs Pamphlet* and the *Yearbook* mentioned above have probably succeeded in familiarizing a great many people with the value of a liberally oriented approach to collegiate business education.

Within the last few years it has become evident that some of the major foundations have become interested in the trend and quality of business education in the United States. The Pierson survey, *The Education of American Businessmen,* was sponsored by the Carnegie Corporation of New York, while the Gordon and Howell study, *Higher Education for Business,* was sponsored by the Ford Foundation.[26] Published in 1959, both of these major works devote considerable attention to the relation between business and liberal arts education. It should be stated that the present study, one of a series relating to liberal education in the professions, was sponsored by the Carnegie Corporation.

Individual colleges have also received financial support in the way of program evaluation. The Ford Foundation helped to sponsor the Educational Survey of the University of Pennsylvania, one phase of which included an appraisal of the Wharton School of Finance and Commerce.

It should also be mentioned that in 1958 the University of Chicago sponsored a "Conference on the Role of the Behavioral Sciences in Business Education," the first of its kind to be held in this country.

---

[24] Shepard, *op. cit.,* p. 27.

[25] *American Business Education Association Yearbook,* Vol. 14 (1957).

[26] Frank C. Pierson, *The Education of American Businessmen* (New York: McGraw-Hill Book Co., 1959). Robert A. Gordon and James E. Howell, *Higher Education for Business* (New York: Columbia University Press, 1959).

Representatives of most of the leading business colleges were in attendance, as were several of the foundation people. Among the topics discussed were a number which pertained to the issue of generalized versus specialized education and the relation of liberal arts—particularly in the behavioral sciences—to business preparation.

And finally, mention should be made of the growth of the American Association of Collegiate Schools of Business. As has been pointed out, one of the membership requirements of this organization is that 40 per cent of the student's work be taken in non-business subjects. Non-member colleges can—and often do—permit their students to take heavy concentrations of specialized business courses. The point is that of all the colleges and universities offering business programs, a minority are members of the A.A.C.S.B. In recent periods, however, the latter organization has grown, both in size and in prestige. In 1931 there were but forty-two member colleges,[27] whereas twenty-five years later the number had grown to eighty-seven.[28] The A.A.C.S.B. has also come to be recognized by the United States Office of Education as the accrediting agency in this field. At any rate, as the number of member-colleges continues to increase, and as the prestige of the organization grows, there should be some tendency for over-specialization in the business areas to decline. Whether the A.A.C.S.B. should do more in the way of liberalization policy will be discussed in the final section.

[27] James Bossard and J. Frederick Dewhurst, *University for Business* (Philadelphia: University of Pennsylvania Press, 1935), pp. 265-266.
[28] "Collegiate Schools of Business," mimeographed release of July 1957, by the U. S. Office of Education, Division of Higher Education.

Chapter 5

CURRENT PROGRAMS IN BUSINESS EDUCATION

NATURE OF RECENT CHANGES

ACTUAL CHANGES IN BUSINESS CURRICULA HAVE PERHAPS LAGGED behind the "change in climate" just discussed. There have nevertheless been perceptible differences in the character of American business education approximately since the beginning of the present decade. No dominant motif has as yet emerged. Yet several important strains appear in the present picture, and each of these symbolizes change in the role and position of liberal education in training for business.

Viewing the current scene very generally, one might conclude that in every important way the inclinations of business educators are to provide for increases and improvement in the liberal education of their students. Thus, while there has been no change in the minimum non-business course requirements for undergraduate schools of business by the American Association of Collegiate Schools of Business, some important schools operating at this undergraduate level have acted to increase the percentage and/or the impact of liberal arts courses taken by their students. Included among these schools are the Northwestern University School of Business, the Wharton School of Finance and Commerce of the University of Pennsylvania, and the Department of Engineering Administration of the Massachusetts Institute of Technology.

At Northwestern the official policy of the School of Business Administration is to encourage liberal arts study by business students. Students are urged to take 50 per cent of their work in liberal arts. In addition, encouragement is given to combined majors, involving business and liberal arts subjects. Cultural breadth is taken to be a primary objective in undergraduate business training.

Similarly, the Wharton School undergraduate curriculum, which was revised in 1961,

> increases the weight given to those social, scientific, and humanistic ideas that are impinging more and more on business judgments.
>
> It accomplishes this partly by enriching the liberal arts ingredients of the student's experience, but more significantly by formulating and adapting these ingredients to fit the particular needs of the prospective business man or woman. The new course of studies recognizes that technical competence, however essential it may be, is no longer enough for effective management; tomorrow's business leaders must be sensitive also to the constant interplay between business policy and the great political, technological, and social forces of the second half of the Twentieth Century.
>
> The main goal of the new curriculum is to provide a program which emphasizes the position of the business leader in society. It is based on the premise that a student who completes the program will possess, not only a solid foundation in business principles and practices, and a special competence in his field of concentration, but also an ability to use the tools of quantitative analysis in the solution of business problems, a proficiency in oral and written communications, a broad understanding of the physical and social sciences and their relationship to business policy and decision making, and an *increased appreciation of the cultural aspects of life together with a deeper awareness of ethical and social values.*[1]

In the undergraduate program of Massachusetts Institute of Technology, business requirements have been confined to minimal exposure in the "functional" and "tool" subjects. Students are required to elect heavily in the humanities, as well as to take certain "general education" courses. While the latter are required of all M.I.T. undergraduates, there is no reason apparent to suggest that this arrangement would be significantly altered in other circum-

[1] University of Pennsylvania, *Undergraduate Catalogue, 1962-1963*, pp. 117-118. (Italics added.)

stances. In a report made concerning the role of the social sciences in the newly created graduate School of Industrial Management, a faculty committee made this observation:

> This is the kind of education we believe the School of Industrial Management should offer. It places the general above the specific, speculation before practice, and seeks the development of understanding rather than training in special skills. It is not, in the narrow meaning of the phrase, a practical education. On the other hand, we have been convinced by the universal testimony of those who appeared before us that it is the most practical way to begin the education of young men who are to deal with the major problems of management. In this connection the School must make perfectly clear to the students that they do not go out wise and experienced executives; they go out to begin at the beginning in industry, where they will continue their education . . . .[2]

These statements suggest another motif in the picture of current business training, namely a revision in the course content of business offerings. Greater emphasis seems now to be placed upon more traditional academic disciplines, e.g., psychology, sociology, and economics, and less upon a description of business practice. Some other possible implications of this change in emphasis for liberal education will be discussed more fully below. For the moment, the fact that liberal arts subjects are involved and also are being invoked as a substitute for obviously functional training suggest possibly a different kind of renaissance for liberal education in business training.

Many business educators seem to feel that liberalization of the business courses, themselves, represents the only satisfactory way of handling the matter of providing liberal education. Thus Oxenfeldt and Sayles of Columbia assert:

> We believe that behavioral sciences should not be presented as "behavioral sciences" but should be built right into the subject matter area of business courses.
>
> Business students' interest and motivation can be gravely dampened if they are exposed to materials prepared for persons whose interest is very different from their own; in addition, difficulties of

[2]Report of the Committee to Consider the Place of the Social Sciences in the School of Industrial Management, Massachusetts Institute of Technology, Cambridge, Mass., June 16, 1952.

vocabulary (pedantic jargon) and viewpoint can consume very large amounts of time, which could be put to far more valuable uses.[3]

It is difficult to measure the effect of these efforts to liberalize business courses. Some notion of the importance of what appears to be a growing trend can be obtained by examining the character of recent faculty appointments in schools of business. With certain notable exceptions, schools of business in the pre-World War II era seemed to look with favor on prospective faculty members whose backgrounds were predominantly in business operation or close to it. Such a pattern still probably exists in certain respects. There seems to be an increasingly tendency, however, to favor the *academic* specialist. Recent faculty additions at the Wharton School, the University of Chicago School of Business, the Carnegie Graduate School of Industrial Administration, and the Massachusetts Institute of Technology School of Industrial Management can be cited as specific examples in this connection. A number of other schools of business also have been appointing practicing economists, psychologists, mathematicians, sociologists, anthropologists, historians, and other academic specialists to their respective faculties.

As a matter of fact, one could argue that in the last decade or so, business organizations have "raided" the business school faculties rather than the other way around. Rare is the business school faculty today which does not have at least some of its members serving as consultants to business. Interestingly enough, when the McKinsey Foundation made its 1962 awards for the five "best management books" of the year, it was discovered that all five were written by professors. Commenting on this fact, *Business Week* raises the question, "Has leadership of the U.S. management movement already passed irretrievably from the professional managers to the professional educators? Or will future book awards some day recognize the experienced management man as an authority in his own field?"[4]

[3] A. R. Oxenfeldt and L. Sayles, "Behavioral Sciences in the Columbia Graduate School of Business," Memorandum to Participants in Conferences on the Behavioral Sciences in Business Schools, University of Chicago, 1958.

[4] "Management Pattern: Some Trophies from the 'Jungle'," *Business Week* (February 16, 1963), p. 140.

Graduate training for business, leading to the M.B.A. degree or its equivalent, is the predominant offering at three of the institutions mentioned above. In two cases—the Carnegie Graduate School of Industrial Administration and the Massachusetts Institute of Technology School of Industrial Management—it is to be noted that such a decision was made within the last decade. As has been observed earlier, there seems generally to have been some growth in the relative importance of graduate business education.

There is a seemingly favorable implication for the future of liberal arts which is to be found in the growth of graduate training, especially when the character of the training is based upon the other disciplines. However, the reasons for certain "conversions" to higher level training for business appear to be complex and in some cases not so clearly oriented to the idea of a liberal education as may appear on the surface. In some cases, the movement of a school of business from the undergraduate level has represented a "strategic retreat" from the pressures of criticisms leveled at business training by the liberal arts faculties of academic institutions. In other cases, the movement to graduate level training has been the result of what might be described as a recognition of the changed "market" for business education. Graduate applications have risen sharply at many schools of business, and there has been a natural diversion of resources to this area of training, especially in cases where faculties have come to include more specialists from the academic disciplines. The fact that graduate applicants have increasingly appeared to be intellectually more gifted than undergraduate applicants has often provided an added incentive to expansion in the graduate area.[5]

Beyond all of these considerations, which might be described as tactical, and which have only indirect significance for the role of liberal arts in business training, is the "change in climate" discussed earlier. It seems clear that some business educators are of the opinion that training for business should be professional in character, as is training for law and medicine, and that this professional training is most appropriately offered to students with baccalaureate degrees.

[5]Cf. Wharton Survey Advisory Committee, *A Program for the Wharton School,* Mimeographed report (Philadelphia: University of Pennsylvania, 1957), p. 22.

The following paragraphs from the catalogue of the University of Chicago School of Business are perhaps most illustrative of this point of view:

> The need today for professional education for business administration is clearly defined and growing constantly. Modern business operations and management demand an increasingly high order of technical knowledge and administrative skill. It is now widely recognized that in business, as in law or engineering or medicine, formal professional education is of vital importance in preparation for a career.
>
> Education for business at the university level offers significant advantages. It conserves time by shortening the period of apprenticeship for higher business responsibilities. It provides a breadth of view and a perspective respecting business activities and problems which is difficult to acquire through practical experience alone. More important, it supplements experience and greatly enhances its worth by supplying the valuable insights of theory and of basic principles of business administration.[6]

The significance of the growth of graduate training in business with respect to the role of liberal education becomes most encouraging in light of such statements of purpose. Otherwise there are questions. In a sense, of course, a movement towards graduate training for any of the reasons which have been cited automatically enhances liberal education simply because the prerequisite undergraduate training still has to take place. All too often, however, the absence of what might be described as purposeful professionalism in the objectives of graduate programs in business is accompanied by the lack of a clear-cut plan for dividing the labor of education as between the undergraduate and the graduate levels.

Thus if one examines the requirements for the M.B.A. degree at schools of business where the graduate program has developed not so much as the result of a design inspired out of consideration of professional concepts as for other reasons, one finds little attention given to the character of undergraduate training. On the other hand, in the case of schools which have developed an M.B.A. program out of explicitly professional considerations there is usually

---

[6] University of Chicago, *Announcements of the Graduate School of Business,* 1956-1957, p. 4.

some notion of relationship between undergraduate and graduate education. Even when a specialized technical background is called for, such as is true in the case of the Carnegie and M.I.T. Schools, special efforts aimed at developing breadth of view are usually attempted through required business offerings of a distinctly non-functional, non-technical nature.

EXECUTIVE TRAINING PROGRAMS

The correlation of the professional viewpoint concerning business education with a realization of the importance of the liberal arts tends to show up especially in some of the recently developed programs for executives. Probably the majority of these programs are still straight "shop," i.e., are concerned with the usual gamut of present-day business school subjects, such as "policy," control, etc. In the last few years, however, there have been some interesting departures from the usual pattern. The Executive Development Program offered by the School of Business of Indiana University includes, for example, courses in "Executive Reading" and "Current Trends in Literature." More extreme was the Institute of Humanistic Studies for Executives, developed at the University of Pennsylvania for the Bell System. The central feature of this program might be described as the reading and discussion of a list of great books.[7] One of the most recent efforts, reported in the *Harvard Business Review,* was the humanities program for executives, sponsored by the Carnegie Institute of Technology.[8]

These and similar developments at other institutions could be cited as a bellweather for business education in the future. Certainly if the business community demands and is willing to pay for liberal arts exposure on the part of its "comers," schools of business might be expected to adjust their curricula at all levels so as to give more place to liberal education. On the other hand, most schools of busi-

[7] Cf., E. Digby Baltzell, "Bell Telephone's Experiment in Education," *Harper's,* Vol. 210 (March 1955), pp. 73-77.

[8] L. Hazard, "Humanities for the Businessman," *Harvard Business Review,* Vol. 38, November 1960, pp. 39-44.

ness are in a somewhat different position regarding their matriculated students as compared with these special groups of executives. The outcome with respect to the position of the liberal arts may well be different in the case of the programs for the former group.

FURTHER ANALYSIS OF CURRENT TRENDS

The substance of what has just been described would seem to be that in a variety of ways schools of business are currently becoming more liberal; that is to say, less specialized and functional, in their educational programs. A good question is whether this is really so. Perhaps the outward symptoms of more liberal arts courses in the curricula, more teachers from the academic disciplines, and an encouragement of liberal education as an integral part of professional training are misleading in terms of the inward realities of the current business education *corpus.*

It is a plausible hypothesis that many of the people who have spoken in favor of what they call liberal education are in the last analysis partisans of changes in business training which are quite clearly illiberal in the essential components. To demand training in "how to get along with people," or in public speaking, is to demand something other than liberal education, no matter what department of a university happens to be in charge of the course or what the course is called.[9]

Does this misunderstanding or, perhaps in some cases, hypocrisy, pervade the new motifs in business education which have been described above? One of the writers talked with a business school dean who, in discussing his reasons for upgrading the role of liberal arts courses in the curriculum of his school, revealed that he was doing so merely to "keep in step" with what he had ascertained to be the attitude of the times. He had no particular feeling about liberal arts courses, pro or con, and he definitely was not thinking in terms of liberal education.

Of significance also is a statement made in a *Business Week*

[9] Cf., William H. White, Jr., "The New Illiteracy," *Saturday Review,* Vol. 36 (November 21, 1953), pp. 33-35.

"roundup" story. According to the article, "every business educator interviewed agreed that business students at the present time need far more training in liberal arts, basic sciences and engineering, social sciences and (especially) communications skills."[10]

It need hardly be mentioned that there are still a good many non-believers among the business educators as far as the values of a heavily liberal arts education for business are concerned:

> It is sometimes said a student can acquire a knowledge of business administration on the job after graduation. No doubt this is true in regard to certain phases of business, particularly techniques. However, the philosophy, history and theoretical principles of a field are hardly learned on the job.[11]

Yet the thought behind the statement quoted is that liberal education may be tendered in business school courses, rather than that liberal education should not be offered. Generally speaking *the current disagreement among business educators would appear to relate to the method of providing liberal education.*

In the matter of the recent growth in emphasis on graduate professional training for business, the prospects for more liberal education as a complement are perhaps not so clear. As has been pointed out already, some schools of business seem to have turned to graduate professional training for reasons of expediency. In so doing they often have *not* devised a self-contained curriculum which either leaves the prospective master's candidate completely free to pursue a liberal education in his undergraduate program or else attempts to compensate for not having done so. The requirements for the master's degree in some of these instances are such as to permit a year's saving in time for the student who has worked into his undergraduate program a rather large number of prerequisites for work at the so-called graduate level in business. Fortunately, some schools have recently started to require resident training in the prerequisites for all students, although it should be said that the reason for this

[10] "Popularity Swamps Business Schools," *Business Week* (December 15, 1956), pp. 193-194.

[11] Cf. Richard E. Mulcahy, "Why a Business College?" *America*, Vol. 98, No. 14 (January 11, 1958), p. 423. Mulcahy, who is Dean of the College of Business Administration of the University of San Francisco, points out, however, that both liberal arts and business courses are relevant and necessary.

change in policy has more often been a desire for uniformity of training in the prerequisites rather than an explicit interest in liberal education at the undergraduate level.

The biggest questions connected with the interpretation of the points which have been described in the preceding section come up in any attempt to assess the hiring by schools of business of academic specialists. As has been stated, many of these people represent traditional liberal arts subjects. On the other hand, the circumstances of their hiring have not always, or even usually, been to provide liberal education.

A number of schools of business, including that of the University of California at Los Angeles and Case Institute's Department of Engineering Administration, have taken on applied mathematicians and physicists expressly to enhance the development of curricula and services of an "operations research" variety. The operations research area is generally concerned with applying advanced techniques for solving business problems. As is well known, schools of business have been rushing to build up programs which fit this general description.

Another reason for the hiring of specialists is to be found in a desire on the part of schools of business to enhance their academic prestige. It will be recalled that schools of business have been roundly criticized for their kind of pragmatism. Much of this criticism has been directed not at the pragmatism but at the quality of the pragmatism. Every academician knows that incompetence is a much more embarrassing charge than is illiberality. On this basis it could be argued that the desire on the part of business schools to achieve academic prestige is a much more important driving force on the current scene than is the desire to turn out broadly educated and literate graduates.

Whether or not the motive of acquiring academic prestige will hurt the cause of liberal education for business students is indeed a moot question. If the specialists are generally assigned to graduate training, as appears to be the practice, there would be little problem unless graduate training for business is conceived to have the same relationship to undergraduate training as seems to hold in some of the academic fields. This does not appear likely.

Also a great deal depends upon the academic specialists themselves. Quite possibly a number of these people will turn out to be much broader in their outlook than their more practically-oriented predecessors and colleagues in the business faculties.

SUMMARY

In this chapter we have dealt with current phases on the business education scene. There are a number of developments which seem to give promise of a more substantial place for liberal education of the business student. Three important changes appear to be: (1) an increased curricular emphasis on liberal arts subjects, (2) an upswing in the recruiting of academically-oriented as opposed to practice-oriented faculty members, and (3) a moderate shift in the relative importance of graduate training with a professional intention.

To what extent these developments have been inspired by a conviction on the part of business educators regarding the value of truly liberal education for business students is not entirely clear. Also an alternative hypothesis might be that the business schools are, as a more basic policy, engaged in a drive to increase their academic prestige. Though other considerations may be more important, the cause of liberal arts may still be enhanced in the present phase of business education by virtue of a decrease in the emphasis on traditional business practice and functions.

Chapter 6

SOME CLOUDS ON THE BUSINESS EDUCATION
HORIZON

IN CHAPTERS 4 AND 5 IT WAS SHOWN THAT IN THE POST-WAR PERIOD
(*a*) a more favorable liberal arts "climate" has emerged with respect
to the administration of business programs, and (*b*) some collegiate
schools of business are expressly turning away from the rather narrowly prescribed, specialized type of business curriculum. At the
same time it must be pointed out that insofar as the amalgamation
of business and liberal education is concerned certain obstacles and
counter forces remain. For instance, ideological differences between
the liberal arts and business faculties has by no means disappeared,
as any one teaching in either field can attest. A case in point is the
article, "The Educational Consequences of Laissez Faire," written
by Lloyd P. Williams for *School and Society*.[1]

Williams contends that business stands for most everything that
liberal education opposes; that "business philosophy has become or-
thodox and, hence, delimits the concept of truth"; that "business en-
courages the teaching of knowledge thought to be 'functional' or
'practical,' and while giving lip service to the liberal studies, finds
little place for them in practice"; that "business would turn physical
education from its proper function into a commercial enterprise";
that "business through advertising supports radio, TV, and the news-
papers, which frequently banalize both news and art, diverts the pub-

[1] Lloyd P. Williams, "The Educational Consequences of Laissez Faire," Vo. 85
(February 2, 1957), pp. 38-39.

lic from more serious considerations, and minimizes the use of these educational facilities for humane and imaginative social purposes." The same writer maintains that business is against critical analysis of existing social institutions, and that without continued self-criticism of this kind our whole societal fabric is undermined. In one of the most biting criticisms since that of Veblen's, Williams goes on to claim that:

> The business orthodoxy being dominant, it allows logically that organized business will set the tolerance limits of really serious social criticism . . . . The inevitable net consequence of an institutionalized and, hence, orthodox laissez faire for the educational community is to distort ideas and sentiments to fit the Procrustean bed of an ac-quisitive morality, to measure efficiency in education by business standards, and to make subject matter a mere device for facilitating expedient action rather than a tool for enhancing individual growth, for social enrichment, and for humane living . . . . Insofar as the business ideology fosters a climate of educational opinion that abets materialism, scientism, and the philosophy of immediacy, it debases that which it touches and renders a disservice to humanity. Assuming the continued growth and extension of knowledge, the continued flowering of the creative spirit and the continued existence of the Judeo-Christian morality, the noxious side of business influence upon education and culture is hardly to be conceived as a permanent part of the social order.[2]

While the foregoing statement can hardly be taken as representative of non-business educators, it is nevertheless ample proof of the animosity that is still harbored by some liberal arts advocates.

Another question that should be raised pertains to the presumed broadening of the business offerings. In a survey of seventy-four business school deans in 1950 and again in 1954, Weldon Taylor, chairman of the marketing department at Brigham Young University, makes some interesting observations.[3] With regard to the question as to what the trend of business education *should* be, 68 per cent of the deans advocated a decrease in the number of professional courses. However, the respondents were evenly divided on the question of whether the trend actually was in this direction.

[2] *Ibid.,* p. 39.
[3] Weldon Taylor, "Are Business Schools Meeting the Challenge?" *Collegiate News and Views,* Vol. 10 (October 1956), pp. 1-6.

Taylor also found that the general business major had increased from 12.6 to 23.1 per cent of the total share of majors, and that the areas of narrow specialty were attracting relatively few majors; e.g., finance and banking, 6 per cent; business law, 1 per cent; and real estate, insurance, transportation, and foreign trade combined, 5 per cent. In conclusion, Taylor states that:

> In reviewing the results of the survey, there is evidence that the student is beginning to choose broadly rather than confine his studies to narrow fields . . . . Most encouraging, also is the fact that the Deans express an almost universal conviction that business education offerings should be more comprehensive and less specialized. From these trends, there is real hope that the American college can be sensitive to the real needs of society and flexible enough to adopt progressive revisions to meet the challenge of change. However, does a broadening of the base of our business school offering to include more of the conventional business school courses provide the breadth in liberal training for which our business leaders are asking? We have no indication in our survey of a change which would encourage the student to expand his areas of awareness to include relationships outside the conventional business subjects, where the solution of many business problems seems to lie. True, we have pointed to a tendency to broaden basic group requirements. But there is still a challenge in the selecting and training of teachers, planning of courses, and establishing administrative goals, patterns, and policies which will envision an ever-broadening area of relationships that are becoming more vital to an enlightened and capable business administrator.[4]

In any discussion relating to the broadening of the business curriculum one very practical question should be raised: Irrespective of the *theoretical* value of liberal business education, what—from the student's viewpoint—is the practical (job-getting and starting-salary) advantage of such a program as compared to one involving specialized business training? Based on the statements of business leaders quoted previously, one might think that the generalist would have a job-market advantage over the specialist. However, as any one who has had experience with personnel recruiters well knows, such is not the case. On the contrary, personnel men who visit college campuses in June are, by and large, looking for specialists in particular business fields like accounting and marketing. The generalist is handicapped

[4] *Ibid.,* p. 6.

by (*a*) the number of jobs available to him, and (*b*) the starting salaries that are offered.

While the above facts are well known to all college and university personnel officers, and presumably to the student bodies, the significance of the matter has not always been realized; namely, that the employment prejudice against the broadly trained man serves as a real obstacle to the adoption of a more liberal educational curriculum.

In an effort to see just what it is that employers are looking for in the way of college-trained men, Hailstones, Roberts, and Steinbruegee conducted a questionnaire survey of personnel managers in the Cincinnati area. The survey revealed, among other things, that insofar as subject matter was concerned, the personnel managers rated specific courses in the following rank order of importance.

1. English
2. Mathematics
3. Business Letter Writing
4. Public Speaking
5. Accounting
6. Industrial Management
7. Labor
8. Business Law
9. Finance
10. Marketing

Subjects such as foreign language, sociology, political science, history, psychology, and science were given relatively low ratings.[5]

What about the contrary statements made by so many of the top business executives? In *The Organization Man,* William H. Whyte makes the following pointed observation:

> This brings us to an interesting anomaly. Lately, leaders of U. S. business have been complaining that there are nowhere near enough "generalists." The average management man, they have been declaring, has been far too narrowly educated . . . . Give us the well-rounded man, business leaders are saying to the colleges, the man steeped in fundamentals; we will give him the specialized knowledge he needs.

[5] T. J. Hailstones, E. E. Roberts, and John Steinbruegee, "Personnel Managers Evaluate a College Business Program," *Collegiate News and Views,* Vol. 8 (May 1955), pp. 7-11.

Convention after convention they make this plea—and their recruiters go right on doing what they've been doing: demanding more specialists. This does not spring from bad faith. The top man may be perfectly sincere in asking for the man with a broad view—he might even be a liberal arts man himself. Somewhere along the line, however, this gets translated and retranslated by the organization people, so that by the time the company gets down to cases the specifications for its officer candidates are something quite different.[6]

Another cloud on the business education horizon relates to the definition of a "broadened" business education. In recent months, for example, there has been much talk of "broadening" the base of business education by the inclusion of behavioral science principles. As was mentioned in the preceding section, however, there is some question as to whether such incorporation is intended to broaden the student's outlook or to make him a more effective cog in the business machine.

And finally, some mention should be made of the official position of the American Association of Collegiate Schools of Business relative to the liberal arts requirement for member colleges. Since 1924 this organization has required that 40 per cent of the student's hours be in non-business subjects. The present regulation reads as follows: "At least forty per cent of the total hours required for the bachelor's degree must be taken in business and economic subjects; the major portion of the courses in this group shall be in business administration. At least forty per cent of the total hours required for the bachelor's degree must be taken in subjects other than business and economics provided that economic principles and economic history may be counted in either the business or nonbusiness groups. With respect to the latter, breadth not specialization is the objective."[7]

The A.A.C.S.B., following the above requirement, has stood against the idea of a narrowly prescribed business education at the expense of the liberal arts. In view of the long-standing liberal arts requirement it is more than a little surprising that, in the minds of many observers at least, business curricula have indeed become over-

---

[6] William H. Whyte, Jr., *The Organization Man* (Garden City, N.Y.: Doubleday and Co., 1956) p. 101.

[7] *Constitution and Standards for Membership* (pamphlet), (St. Louis, Mo.: American Association of Collegiate Schools of Business, 1962), p. 3.

specialized. On the surface, the 40-40-20 ratio seems to be an equit-
able arrangement. On the other hand, this particular requirement
has remained unchanged for almost forty years, and has not allayed
the chronic charge of overspecialization. In view of this fact, and
in view of the fact that the over-all business environment has changed
radically since the early 1920's, it may be that a policy reassessment
is in order.

Chapter 7

BUSINESS EDUCATION AT THE CROSSROADS

IT SEEMS QUITE CLEAR FROM THIS SURVEY THAT THE POTENTIAL role of the liberal arts in training for business is very great. Recent statements by both business men and educators give substantial emphasis to the notion of a broadened educational base in business training. As Gordon and Howell point out in their recent survey, "Businessmen in the decades ahead will need a higher order of analytical ability, a more sophisticated skill, *a greater capacity to deal with the external environment of business, and more of an ability to cope with rapid change than has been true in the past."*[1]

The growth of graduate business training, as well as the recent efforts of a number of leading undergraduate business schools to provide more liberal arts work for their students, suggest that an important break with past philosophies of preparing students for business may be occurring at the present time.

Some other current data, however, cast doubt on the wisdom of extrapolating very far in this direction. One of the most important of these harder facts is the continuing preference exhibited by company personnel officers for students with highly specialized training. If liberal arts graduates are slighted in the job market, students in general can hardly be expected to cooperate in any liberalization of training for business. And such cooperation is necessary, even in a "sellers' market" for education.

[1] Robert A. Gordon and James E. Howell, *Higher Education for Business* (New York: Columbia University Press, 1959), p. 127. (Italics added.)

The attitude of the higher echelons of American business leadership also raises some questions, despite the usual protestations of affection for the liberal arts. Close scrutiny of some of the statements which have been made by business leaders suggests that what is really wanted is more training in specific skills currently taught in liberal arts departments of our collegiate institutions. If this is true, then of course the future of the essentially non-functional type of education which we call liberal arts is not quite so bright as it may now seem.

Finally it is to be noted that, since World War II, many schools of business have been favoring academic specialists in their staff appointments, a trend which by 1963 has become fully apparent to all concerned. Quite possibly these academicians will prove to be much more favorable towards the liberal arts than their more "action-oriented" predecessors. Nevertheless, one wonders whether or not a new specialization is being substituted for an old one. Without a doubt the technical level of the training will be higher than it has been, but this is no guarantee of the education being liberal.

In view of these problems, as well as of the past history of the relationship between the liberal arts and business preparation, the writers would like to advance five ideas as being helpful to the cause of providing a liberal education for business. The first of these is that schools of business and their respective liberal arts counterparts at our collegiate institutions stop the internecine warfare which has seemed to continue endlessly throughout the years and which does not seem to have accomplished very much in the matter of advancing the cause of either business or liberal education. It would seem at this point in the history of the battle that more is to be gained by constructive criticism which takes into consideration the realities and needs of business education than by attempts to obliterate the very thought of *either* business *or* liberal arts education.

A second idea is that the American Association of Collegiate Schools of Business should perhaps reassess its provisions regarding the ratio of business to liberal arts course content. Despite the fact that since 1925 when the A.A.C.S.B. curriculum provisions were promulgated, 60 per cent of the training of a business student can be in liberal arts subjects, few persons, including business educators, seem satisfied that the average business school graduate is a liberally educated individual.

Third, it would seem desirable for more schools in various parts of the country to consider business education as professional training coming after an undergraduate course emphasizing liberal arts values. As Gordon and Howell point out:

> In the coming decades there is every likelihood that graduate programs, certainly in terms of total enrollments and probably in relation to undergraduate work, will become still more important. At many of the older schools this shift in emphasis is already well under way, as new schools have come into the undergraduate field . . . .
>
> Of seventy-six schools with graduate programs which supplied the necessary data, fifty-three estimated that their graduate enrollment would increase twice or more by 1970, while thirty-one projected an increase of three times or more. Projections of undergraduate and graduate enrollments to 1970 at schools offering work at both levels indicate that graduate enrollment will increase more than twice as fast.[2]

The fact remains, however, that as of early 1963 there were only some dozen schools of business which offer *only* graduate training. Continuing the above quotation, Gordon and Howell state that, with regard to over-all graduate business education,

> At present, graduate work is largely concentrated at a small group of institutions, with nine schools granting 57 per cent of all master's degrees and 50 per cent of all doctoral degrees. (These nine schools are: Chicago, Columbia, Harvard, Indiana, Michigan, Northwestern, New York University, Stanford, and Wharton.)[3]

Obviously, not all business schools should attempt to enter the graduate bailiwick. Gordon and Howell caution that "Business schools should not endeavor to offer advanced degree programs unless they have the resources needed for high-quality work."[4] Nevertheless, in view of the rather restricted number of high-quality graduate business programs, and in further view of the geographical disproportion involved, existing schools of business should be giving more thought to the undergraduate/graduate ratio.

[2] *Ibid.,* pp. 229-230.
[3] *Ibid.*
[4] *Ibid.*

Fourth, every effort should be made to liberalize the content of the prevailing undergraduate business programs. Whether such liberalization would be best accomplished through more offerings in the liberal arts, or through direct change within the business courses themselves probably depends upon conditions existing at a particular institution. In the very nature of academic and bureaucratic reality, such would almost have to be the case. Simply in terms of a personal judgment, the present writers feel that the values and orientation of the teacher are more important than whether the course in question is nominally a business or a liberal arts offering.

The writers' fifth and, in their estimate, most important recommendation is that an attempt should be made, once and for all, to "pin down" the executives and personnel recruiters who reportedly say one thing and do another with respect to liberal education for business. To paraphrase William H. Whyte, American business leaders keep crying out for well-rounded, liberally-trained graduates —generalists rather than specialists—and their recruiters go right on doing what they've been doing: demanding and hiring more specialists![5]

Our thought is not that the business schools should take their cue from the business community but that the business leaders, when called upon to account for the seeming inconsistency between their words and their subordinates' actions, will perhaps undertake to reassess their personnel policies with the goal of providing commensurate openings for the broadly-educated undergraduate.

No one who has thought seriously about the nature of responsibility in business can dispute the desirability of an education in some breadth for those who are being schooled for business responsibility. It is this natural sequence, plus a certain amount of faith in the rationality of both business and educational leaders, which has led the writers to advance the ideas expressed herein and to explore further the elusive role of liberal arts in collegiate preparation for business.

[5] William H. Whyte, Jr., *The Organization Man* (Garden City, N.Y.: Doubleday and Co., 1956), p. 101.

Chapter 8

COLLEGIATE SCHOOLS OF BUSINESS:
A FURTHER APPRAISAL*

THIS CHAPTER IS LIMITED TO A CONSIDERATION OF UNDERGRADUATE schools of business. This restriction rests on the conviction that, even though existing graduate schools of business which accept only students with bachelor's degrees may represent the wave of the future, this wave is no great roller that will immediately submerge the undergraduate enterprises. In the years ahead, most young people who enter business from an institution of higher education will, and should, have obtained their education in four undergraduate years, or preferably in three. Since the four-year undergraduate curriculum in which general and professional subject matter are combined in varying proportions as the student proceeds toward the bachelor's degree has been justified elsewhere, no additional defense of these curricular arrangements is considered necessary at this point.[1]

The title of this chapter contains two words which presuppose a point of reference. "Further" implies going beyond an earlier assessment. Many who have played a part in, or employed the graduates of, collegiate schools of business will recall two reports issued several years ago which evaluated these institutions.[2] These comprehensive

* By Earl J. McGrath.

[1] See Earl J. McGrath, *Liberal Education in the Professions* (New York: Bureau of Publications, Teachers College, Columbia University, 1959), pp. 50-59.

[2] Robert A. Gordon and James E. Howell, *Higher Education for Business* (New York: Columbia University Press, 1959); Frank C. Pierson, *The Education of American Businessmen* (New York: McGraw-Hill Book Co., 1959).

studies rightly attracted nationwide attention and they have already been followed by, if not caused, some commendable reforms in policy and practice in collegiate education for business.

The current appraisal, though it does treat some of the concepts contained in these reports, stems from a longer association with, and study of, the purposes and programs of schools of business—an association which began in the late twenties at the University of Buffalo and concluded only in the late fifties at the University of Kansas City. Moreover, this assessment rests on a prolonged study of the more comprehensive purposes of our system of higher education as it has attempted to serve a society whose social, economic, and cultural life has changed with increasing swiftness.

The most recent such study is reflected in a series of analyses of a variety of undergraduate professional schools conducted by the Institute of Higher Education. Hence, even though some adversions may be made to the two recent studies in business, and some questions raised concerning the possible long-run impact of their recommendations, these remarks should not be interpreted as appraisals of appraisals, but rather as independent judgments about very significant aspects of education for careers in business. In any event, the word "further" merely implies that one person is adding his own studied observations on business education to a host of others which reach back at least to the founding of the Wharton School in 1881.

The other word in this title, "appraisal," also implies a point of reference. Some value, standard, or goal must be set before an evaluation can be made. Schools of business can be, and sometimes have been, evaluated in accordance with a variety of criteria. A "good" school may be considered one which employs only faculty members who hold the Ph.D. degree. The excellence of an institution could also be thought to be determined by the percentage of students admitted from the upper quarter of their high school graduating classes, or the number who achieved a score of 600 on the College Entrance Board Examinations. These examples are enough to establish the point that though many criteria may be used to define "good" business education, they are all really irrelevant to the main issue. Excellence in a school of business must in the last analysis be determined by its success in preparing young people as perfectly as possible for a great variety of occupations in the business enterprise. This conception undergirds all the reasoning which follows. In abstract discussion this idea may generally be accepted as obvious, but in practice it is often violated or disregarded.

To be sure, schools of business share certain characteristics with other types of institutions, but these qualities can not be used as distinctive measures of excellence. A school of business may, for example, provide a superior liberal education for its students, but a liberal arts college should be able to do this as well or better. The business faculty may do distinguished research and issue commendable publications, but in this respect many graduate departments of economics could match or surpass it. A school of business may offer high quality and comprehensive instruction in the behavioral sciences, but this would not distinguish it because other university divisions could excel in this respect. Other examples of misplaced emphasis could easily be found. But the justifications for, and the assessment of, these institutions must be based on more specific criteria directly related to the needs of American business. If these institutions cannot meet these differentiating criteria, they really have no reason for existence. Some of the recommendations recently made, if adopted, might cause schools of business to turn out liberally educated graduates, well grounded in the behavioral sciences, possessed of the habits of scholarship, highly intelligent, and yet they might be no better prepared for a career in business than if they had attended a liberal arts college. In this case, whatever its other contributions, such a school of business would have no special justification for being. Some apparently would consider this development desirable, but if the elimination of the undergraduate curriculum in business is their objective, they ought forthrightly to say so, so that the objectives of the dialogue on this subject can be kept clear before the participants.

In terms of the business enterprise, what then are the peculiar functions of an undergraduate school of business? Three major purposes should shape its principal features. They are first, to provide the general, non-professional education essential to business competence, informed citizenship, and an effective personal life; second, to lay down the foundation of general, professional education commonly referred to as "the core," essential for an understanding of the business and industrial enterprise as a whole and for flexible movement within the range of occupations it affords; and third, to initiate the specialized education which enables a graduate immediately to enter an occupation of his own choosing. With each of these three elements in proper proportion and balance, and, of course, with instruction of suitable quality, graduates of schools of business ought to be able not only to get a reasonably good beginning job, but to have acquired as well the abilities and the attitudes essential to future occupational growth and advancement.

If these abstract ideas are translated into concrete terms, a satisfactory undergraduate curriculum in business would consist roughly of 50 per cent, general; 25 per cent, core; and 25 per cent, specialized instruction. Converted into the conventional requirement of 120 credit hours for the bachelor's degree this would mean 60 hours, general; 30 hours, core; and 30 hours, specialized instruction with some local variations depending on faculty attitudes, student interests, and the particular major involved. This weighting appears practically feasible and educationally defensible.

How does existing practice compare with these figures? Recent and comprehensive information on this subject is supplied by Professors Opulente and Clark of St. John's University. During the fall they systematically collected data from nearly 100 of the major schools of business concerning changes which have occurred since the publication of the two reports in 1959. Since that year there has been a significant change in regard to the 50 per cent of general or non-professional subjects proposed above. In 1959, 28.8 per cent of the colleges reporting required from 40 to 49 credits in non-business subjects; by 1962 that percentage had dropped to 9.3, but while in 1959 only 26.6 per cent required as much as 60 to 69 hours of liberal arts and science subjects, by 1962 the percentage in this category had risen to 52.5, and another 38.6 per cent required from 50 to 59 credits. These figures show that more than half of the schools have already reached the standard of 50 per cent in liberal arts and sciences and many others closely approach it.

Correspondence with twenty-five selected schools in November of 1962 disclosed that many are still earnestly trying to redesign their programs to reach the 50 per cent mark. Hence, the situation really looks very encouraging. Moreover, other studies of the Institute of Higher Education show that if some liberal arts courses were genuinely liberal rather than specialized preparatory instruction for future majors, many professional schools would move more decisively toward a larger requirement in these subjects.

The so-called General Business Core, that is, courses required of all business students irrespective of their majors, has also become a more prominent element in the average curriculum. In 1959, 25.4 per cent of the institutions required from 20 to 29 credits. This percentage has now dropped to 16.9 and the requirements above 39 hours have become more common. The percentage required in the core is somewhat higher than that here proposed, but it should be remembered that three to six hours would commonly be devoted to the first course in a subject in which the student later specializes. Moreover, since the core courses are general introductions to the various basic subjects they provide a desirable vocational flexibility, and, therefore, where excessive, they constitute less of a handicap than too many courses in a major field.

The most impressive curricular alteration has occurred in the number of credits required in the major. In 1959, 24.0 per cent of the schools required from 10 to 19 hours; in 1962, this figure had jumped to 55.1 per cent, more than double. On the other hand, few institutions (12.2 per cent) today require more than 29 hours for a major. Only 20.3 per cent reach the percentage of courses in the major suggested as defensible, namely, one quarter of the curriculum. This trend toward a reduction in the major may go too far; in fact, it may reach a point where no major in the conventional sense is really offered.

Those acquainted with developments in business curricula will recognize present trends as mere continuations of those visible for the past quarter century. *One could sum up the general curricular situation by saying that the trends have been toward more general education in the liberal arts and sciences, an increase in the core of business subjects, and a decided drop in the number of credits in the specialized field.*

As far as the future education of young people preparing for careers in business is concerned, there are three other matters of a more general nature which may be of even greater significance than the foregoing curricular changes. The first concerns the percentage of the faculty holding the doctor's degree. A questionnaire prepared by Dean Gilliland of Temple University and recently returned by sixty-one institutions provides illuminating information on this subject. The results reveal a change in the percentage of those holding doctor's degrees from one college in which 13 per cent fewer of the full-time faculty had received this degree to another in which the percentage had risen by 45. The average increase was 15 per cent.

From these figures most scholars would immediately infer that undergraduate business education had automatically improved as a result of this increase in the proportion of the faculty having the doctor's degree. In a measure this would be a valid deduction. These figures might be assumed to imply that on the average, faculty members now know more about their special subjects, have a keener awareness and understanding of the value of scholarship and research, and would, therefore, *ipso facto* be better teachers. Insofar as undergraduate students are concerned, however, the validity of the latter inference has never been objectively demonstrated. On the contrary, as an article in the September 1962 issue of *Horizon*[3] shows, holders of the Ph.D. are becoming so preoccupied with research, writing, and consultation that even if their teaching ability is enhanced through advanced graduate study and research (a questionable assumption), their interest in and dedication to undergraduate teaching dwindles. More and more, faculties in schools of business are attaining the doctor's degree and in turn launching graduate programs. In view of what has already happened in the liberal arts colleges and elsewhere, however, one cannot be called an alarmist or anti-intellectual if he points out that without proper safeguards an increase in the number of Ph.D.'s on the faculty may, whatever other advantages it provides, lead to poorer rather than better undergraduate teaching.

Second, consider the controversial matter of undergraduate specialization in a major. This problem has two facets. One con-

[3] Robert Bendiner, "The Non-Teachers," *Horizon* (September 1962), p. 14.

cerns the question whether undergraduates in business should be permitted to concentrate in a single subject as liberal arts colleges usually require their students to do. Practically the questions is, "Should there be majors in such fields as insurance, retailing, and advertising?" The other question relates to the degree of specialization which should be permitted, that is, the number of hours that the student ought appropriately be allowed to take within a particular field. These are quite different questions. On the extent of specialization the view has already been expressed that not more than 25 per cent of the total curriculum should be devoted to the major and often the proportion might be smaller. Some institutions have imposed grievous handicaps on students by permitting them to take 50 or 60 hours in a single field such as finance, insurance, or management. Institutions following this practice are vulnerable on three grounds—it narrows the student's general education, it thins out the subject matter of his specialty, and it gives him a false sense of having arrived professionally. Thirty to 32 hours ought to be adequate preparation in any major, and in some, fewer hours would be adequate.

But the other question as to whether more than three or four majors, or any at all, ought to be offered can only be answered in terms of the types of jobs for which the institution offers preparation, the changing character of our commercial and industrial enterprise and the opportunity for employment within it, and the value of deep penetration of a field of learning as part of an undergraduate education.

First, consider whether schools of business ought to prepare students only or primarily for top management and upper level executive positions. Some of the statements made by some schools of business as well as by persons who study them to the effect that their curricula ought primarily to train executives or top managers at best exhibit naiveté and at worst duplicity. As Leonard S. Silk has convincingly shown, in the industrial and business enterprise as a whole there are only about 100,000 executives in firms of more than 100 employees, and not all of these by any means are or will in the visible future be graduates of schools of business.[4] Many hold

[4]Leonard S. Silk, *The Education of Businessmen* (New York: Committee for Economic Development, 1960), p. 11.

degrees from liberal arts colleges, engineering schools, law schools, even pharmacy and medical schools in certain firms, and not a few come up through the ranks without a higher education. Yet the number of graduates of schools of business in June 1961 was 50,559.

It follows from these hard facts, as common sense would suggest, that many graduates of schools of business are not going to be top managers—nor should they, any more than all graduates of schools of medicine should expect to become a Sir William Osler or all graduates of law schools, a Blackstone or Storey. This statement contains a good deal of deliberate hyperbole to highlight the pretentious fancifulness of suggesting that all graduates of schools of business should be encouraged to expect to rise to top management jobs. The implication is disturbing that if a man has not risen to a high management position, however successful he may have become in a lower or different job, he has to a degree failed occupationally. Leonard Silk's conclusion seems sound that:

> . . . it would seem rather vain to pretend that the dominant mission of our 163 business schools and our more than 400 departments and divisions of business administration is to turn out hundreds of thousands of wise, gifted, sensitive but tough-skinned, visionary but practical, cultivated and responsible and highly motivated and ambitious but thoughtful and moderate and statesmanlike leaders of American business.[5]

Some graduates who have no capacity for or, more importantly, no interest in the activities of management may still be highly successful in non-directive occupations. They ought not be deluded by seductive literature, or psychologically coerced by invidious statements, away from what would otherwise be economically rewarding and psychically satisfying occupations. A large percentage of undergraduates ought to receive enough liberal and general business education to enable them to move around occupationally at suitable levels without cultivating the patently false notion that they will, or should want to, become president, or even fifth vice president, of the company. This is not to say that schools of business should set

[5] Leonard S. Silk, "New Dimensions in Education and Business," an address before the Association of State Universities and Land-Grant Colleges, Division of Business Administration, Washington, D. C., November 14, 1962.

their sights exclusively on positions below the upper executive levels. Moreover, emphasis in undergraduate schools should be on the type of education which will ensure future occupational growth and the potential for advancement, but the program should recognize that management is only one type of occupation in our society for which schools of business ought to prepare their students.

The other facet of the matter is that until automation completely eliminates the need for special knowledge and skills other than those connected with the operation of machines and equipment many young people ought to be prepared for specialized positions below the level or outside the sphere of management. Our economy is complex. Particular jobs requiring a higher education increase at the rate of ten to twenty a year and institutions of higher education ought to fit young people for them. Pierson lists an aggregate of twenty-three major subjects offered in 1955-1956 in ninety-eight schools.[6] He also reports some obviously questionable courses such as *Hotel Front Office Procedures* and *Principles of Baking: Cookies,* which patently do not belong in a credit program in higher education.

If the amount of specialization in the major is limited to 20 or 25 per cent of the whole, and if the intellectual content and methodology of instruction reflect the putative standards of college and university instruction generally, a considerable variety of majors can be justified. In fact, such a concentration should be of real value to the individual and to industry. As far as the individual is concerned a definite occupational goal and instruction related to it increase motivation to learn and serve as a focal point for the integration of the whole learning experience. Howard Mumford Jones, for many years Professor of English at Harvard, in speaking of the value of an early vocational choice and an organization of the curriculum toward it has the following to say:

> It is wonderful how, when the individual establishes such a goal, education comes into focus. The postponement of the necessity for such a decision by two years has led the student aimlessly through freshman and sophomore courses unrelated to each other and meaningless to him, since his understandable attitude is that they are patiently to be endured until he is permitted to begin his real education.

[6]Pierson, *op. cit.,* p. 219.

But if from the beginning of his college work—indeed, if possible, before beginning that work—the student is faced with the necessity of making an adult choice of occupation, it soon becomes possible for the college to deal with him as an adult. His professional or vocational training will not then be crowded into the last two years of a four-year curriculum, and his "liberal" education will not be administered in the vast and shoreless void of two years of drift; on the contrary, the two can be administered together, the practical necessities of the one will focus the theoretical implications of the other, and the deeper the student plunges into his professional or vocational work the more clearly he will see the necessity of a governing philosophy.[7]

But many of Professor Jones' colleagues in liberal arts departments who argue incontinently for a 30-, 40-, or even 50-hour concentration in such subjects as physics, English, and economics, as indispensable elements in a higher education, strangely seem to find specialization in finance, insurance, or retailing corruptive of sound educational principles.

If depth of study of a subject has value in one field it follows *a priori* that it has value in another. Thomas L. Norton, former dean at New York University School of Commerce, Accounts, and Finance, has made a strong case for the contribution of a major specialization to undergraduate education in business. "Specialization," he says,

> in any one of the broad areas of business permits the student, through sequential courses, to study a subject deeply. He can begin to grasp intelligently the problems of the subject and to apply to them all the interrelationships and analytical skills inherent in the various courses in the Business base as well as those of the General Education part of his curriculum. He has little opportunity of doing this in the Business base courses, because in each he is dealing with only the elementary aspects of the subject . . . .
>
> In my judgment, a specialization of from 18 to 24 credits need not result in exposing the student to "narrow, stultifying instruction," as Pierson contends. To me, this comes pretty close to begging the question. There is no reason to believe a specialization need be narrow or stultifying in an area of business any more than in chemistry or history in a liberal arts college. Assuming that the business courses

[7] Howard Mumford Jones, *Education and World Tragedy* (Cambridge, Mass.: Harvard University Press, 1946), p. 95.

are of high intellectual content and that the desirable combination of courses may come from several disciplines, a field of specialization can make a valuable contribution to the student's intellectual growth.[8]

And the fact that a person fails to remain in his initial type of work for life or even for a year is of little significance. Educationally he has to start somewhere, and if the courses composing a major specialization are taught analytically and in terms of general principles, he should possess the body of knowledge and the complement of intellectual abilities prerequisite to occupational mobility. A single institution should not extend itself too thinly by offering too many specializations, but assuming that the major is kept within a quarter or less of the total program and that the quality of instruction is defensible, the company of schools of business as a whole can appropriately offer any number of specializations. Indeed this is the established pattern of higher education even in undergraduate and graduate liberal arts departments. A study by the Institute of Higher Education reveals that in addition to the conventional majors in such subjects as mathematics, history, and philosophy, independent liberal arts colleges offer several dozen other specialized programs with a more obvious vocational goal such as medical technology, journalism, and accounting. Yet, the Opulente and Clark study shows an aggregate loss since 1959 of 22 majors among the institutions studied. Unless the original offerings were of inferior quality (in which case *no specialty* of any kind should have been offered anyway) even in such established subjects as finance, accounting, or economics, it is a question whether the business community or individual students have been well served by this curricular reorientation. The conception that the number of undergraduate specializations in business should be greatly contracted is supported neither by social need nor by pedagogical principle. Considering schools of business administration as a group, the needs of students indicate the desirability of reversing this trend.

Finally, there is the question of admission standards. Many of the schools queried on this subject provided no answers. Of those which did reply some have raised the qualitative requirements for

[8] Thomas L. Norton, *The Undergraduate Business Curriculum*, The Ford and Carnegie Reports, privately printed.

admission, but many have not. Several studies have shown that some schools of business have accepted students of low scholastic aptitude. Moreover, there is a minimum of ability and high school accomplishment without which respectable higher education becomes impossible, and those who fall below these levels ought to be excluded.

But the recent blind preoccupation with academic excellence throughout the enterprise of higher education may be socially, educationally, and morally indefensible in a democratic society, and wasteful of our human resources to boot. To a considerable extent this obsessive desire to be certain that only the "best" are admitted to our institutions of higher education springs from non-educational forces such as fear of the Russians, a false conception of educational and human worth, a narrow view of academic accomplishment, and plain academic status seeking.

As we review admissions practices, we ought to keep three factors in the forefront of our thinking. First, throughout our history many persons of only modest academic ability have been admitted to our institutions of higher education and have later made good both in college and in life. Because of the unfortunately growing tendency to stress sheer speed of the acquisition of factual knowledge rather than growth in genuine intellectual power, such persons of limited talent and even some of greater aptitude will encounter difficulty in gaining admission to, or remaining in, an institution of higher education.

As we become more mechanically selective in our admissions policies we ought to be careful that we do not disadvantage potentially capable and worthy citizens. Anyone who made the necessary effort could compile an arresting list of distinguished men and women in all activities of life whose high school records were not above, and were frequently below average. Dr. George B. Smith of the University of Kansas, in a study of student careers has discovered that many who stood in the lower half of their high school classes achieved successful and often distinguished records in the university.[9] Even at rather high levels of ability remarkable differences in achievement occur among professional students of differing aptitude and

[9] George Baxter Smith, "Who Would be Eliminated?" *A Study of Selective Admission to College, Kansas Studies in Education,* Vol. 7, No. 1a (December 1956).

previous academic preparation. A recently released study at McGill Medical School reveals no relationship between academic grades and later success in medical practice as indicated by the ratings of members of the profession.[10]

Mr. Henry S. Coleman, Director of College Admissions at Columbia College, in commenting on the predictive value of test scores in the entering class of September, 1961, said that high College Board scores sometimes could be misleading. "Most of the fifteen freshmen," said Mr. Coleman, "with the poorest mid-semester grades scored well on their entrance board examinations. The difference between a boy who scored a high 500 on his examination and one who scored in the low 700's is often negligible."

One ought not conclude from these and other studies that every Tom, Dick, and Harry should be admitted to a school of business or an engineering school, college of liberal arts, or any other university division. But they suggest that (*a*) admissions policies ought to take into consideration factors other than high school records and test scores; (*b*) until more reliable knowledge has been produced on the relationships existing between aptitude and achievement scores and success in various business occupations, a latitudinarian admissions policy is indicated; and (*c*) the admissions policies of any division of a university ought not automatically determine those of any other division. Some have asserted that certain schools of business are the havens of the unfit, the poorly motivated, and the country club set. A Gresham's law probably prevails in schools on a particular campus, and also a kind of molecular attraction doubtless draws together a body of poor or good students, but adequate safeguards can be taken against a gravitation of the inadequately prepared toward any particular school without excluding those who with stimulating teaching could succeed.

Second, since the nation needs a massive corps of men and women in business and industry of widely varying abilities and special skills, educational programs ought to be diversified even in terms of the average aptitude of the students involved. Certain jobs,

[10] R. C. A. Hunter, J. G. Sohrenge, and A. E. Schwartzman, "A Fifteen-Year Follow Up Study of Medical Graduates," *The Canadian Medical Association Journal,* Vol. 87 (October 20, 1962), pp. 865-68.

even those which require a higher education, can be filled with complete competence by those of less than brilliant scholastic promise. In fact, persons of high ability and accomplishment often become badly adjusted in their employments and fail, while others of a different level and type of ability succeed. The need for greater diversity will increase. Moreover, the temper of our people suggests that they will not permit their sons and daughters who do not possess I.Q.'s of 150 to be herded into technical institutes, junior colleges, or segregated courses for the average student. Many such students can profit from four years of business (or other) education within the atmosphere of a college or university, and they will not be denied it by academic snobbishness or a rigid division of academic labor.

In approaching the problem of admissions, as well as of later academic performance, it would be well to recall the thoughtful observation of one of America's wisest educational statesmen, Lotus D. Coffman, for twenty years President of the University of Minnesota, who said on this subject, "It should be remembered that the significance of a college lies not in what students bring to it but in what they take away."[11] Consistent with our traditional social and educational philosophy, schools of business ought to remain considerably diversified in their missions, in their programs, and in the quality of their student clienteles. The result will be an untidy enterprise of business education, but the unparalleled strength of American higher education has been the consequence largely of a belligerent institutional independence. Recent pronouncements would suggest that we abandon all three of the foregoing practices and substitute a more common set of purposes, a more standard curriculum, and more uniform admissions practices. Neither in education for business nor for any other occupation would such actions be in the national interest and even though some weaknesses which ought to be corrected may exist in business education, as in all other kinds, we ought jealously to guard the traditions of independence and variation under which our system of higher education has flourished and served a democratic society better than any other in the world.

[11] Lotus D. Coffman, *The State University, Its Work and Problems* (Minneapolis: University of Minnesota Press, 1934), p. 93.

The views expressed in these chapters have been directed principally to members of the profession, to employers of the graduates of schools of business, and to the public generally. A brief statement needs to be addressed directly to those charged with the responsibility of accrediting schools of business. The present situation at home and abroad demands the maximum development and use of our human resources of all varieties, levels, and complexions. All of us engaged in education, therefore, have the responsibility to favor policies and practices which seem calculated to achieve this goal.

Through the years accrediting organizations have rendered incalculable service in improving the quality of higher education. In the light of the present condition, they can most effectively continue their high service not only by permitting, but by encouraging the greatest possible variation in educational effort, by countenancing wide deviation from what may appear to be sound practice, by not only tolerating but by actually fostering the most radical educational experimentation of all types, and most importantly of all, by imposing inflexible standards only when they are sustained by completely objective and indisputable evidence. By doing so, an accrediting agency will be nourishing healthy educational development in our schools of business, and it will be acting in accordance with our most cherished intellectual traditions of easy accessibility to education and institutional independence.

This book has attempted to review the historical development of the relationships between professional instruction in business and the more general liberal arts subjects. As in the cases of other professions, it has been shown that there has been a steady increase in the latter portions of the curriculum and a decrease in narrow technical instruction related to a particular job. Typically, half the undergraduate's program consists of study in the liberal arts and sciences. This instruction is buttressed by general studies in the field of business. Undergraduate schools almost invariably offer at least several majors, but the aggregate number of specialties has recently declined. This change in policy and practice deserves continuing appraisal in the light of the needs of the individual student, business enterprise, and the nation. All three will be better served by a continuance of wide institutional differences in student selection, in curricula offered, and in faculty preparation than by a rigid imposition of common standards throughout the programs in education for business. In any event, recent recommendations for curriculum reform need to be reappraised in terms of their impact on students and on the educational programs designed to serve them. Schools of business are at a historic crossroads. There is considerable evidence that, through the years, they have, in the best sense of the word "quality," become better institutions. This they can continue to do not by the uncritical adoption of uniform standards, but rather through careful objective appraisals of the value of various types of education for business provided within the flexible framework of our free enterprise system in American higher education.

SELECTED BIBLIOGRAPHY

A. PUBLICATIONS RELATING TO THE ORIGIN AND DEVELOPMENT OF COLLEGIATE BUSINESS EDUCATION

1. BOOKS AND MONOGRAPHS

American Council on Education, *Business Education at the College Level.*
American Council on Education Studies, Series 1. Reports of Committees of the Council No. 7. Washington, D.C.: The Council, 1939.
Prepared by a subcommittee of the A.A.C.S.B., this article contains a historical sketch of collegiate business schools, including a statement on problems and objectives as of 1939.

Haynes, Benjamin, and Harry Jackson, *A History of Business Education in the United States.* Cincinnati, Ohio: South-Western Publishing Co., 1935.
Written by two business educators, this volume covers the earlier history of business education in the U. S., with separate chapters devoted to high schools, private schools, junior colleges, and university schools of business (Ch. VIII).

Hofstadter, Richard, and C. DeWitt Hardy, *The Development and Scope of Higher Education in the United States.* New York: Columbia University Press, 1952.
Prepared at the behest of the Commission on Financing Higher Education, this volume traces the development of the various branches of higher education in the U. S. One section is devoted to the development of business schools, and of the trend of certain liberal arts materials within these schools.

Johnson, Emory R., *The Wharton School—Its First Fifty Years*. Philadelphia: The University of Pennsylvania's Wharton School, 1931.

A thorough-going history of the famed Wharton School's early period, including a discussion of both philosophical and bureaucratic problems.

Knepper, Edwin G., *A History of Business Education in the United States*. Ann Arbor, Mich.: Edwards Brothers, 1941.

A comprehensive history of the development and trends of business education prior to World War II.

Lyon, Leverett S., *Education for Business*. Chicago: University of Chicago Press, 1922 and 1931.

A mammoth volume covering historical and curricular development of business education up to 1930.

Prickett, A. L., *Collegiate Schools of Business in American Education*. Cincinnati, Ohio: South-Western Publishing Co., 1945.

The former Dean of the Business School, Indiana University, gives a well-written account of the development and implications of collegiate education for business.

————, and H. V. Olsen, *The Collegiate Schools of Business in American Education, Third Annual Delta Pi Epsilon Lecture*. Cincinnati, Ohio: South-Western Publishing Co., 1944.

A monograph devoted to the development of collegiate business education, appropriate objectives, types of programs, and standards of the A.A.C.S.B.

Scovill, H. T., *50 Years of Education for Business at the University of Illinois*. Urbana: University of Illinois Press, 1952.

A thorough history, in readable style, of business education at the University of Illinois.

U. S. Office of Education, *Earned Degrees Conferred by Higher Educational Institutions, 1959–1960*. Washington, D.C.: U. S. Government Printing Office, Circular No. 687 (1962).

The yearly U. S. Office of Education report giving statistical breakdowns of degrees in higher education.

2. PERIODICALS AND ARTICLES

Benninger, L. J., "Trends in the Development of Higher Education for Business," *American Business Education Association Yearbook, 1957*, pp. 47-52.

A Professor of Accounting at the University of Florida discusses recent business education trends relative to enrollment, curricula expansion, training for executive leadership, etc.

Crosbaugh, Clyde J., "Objectives of Collegiate Business Education," *Journal of Business Education,* 21: 16-18, February 1946.

The author has analyzed the college catalogues of A.A.C.S.B. members, and attempts a systematic classification of educational goals.

Danskin, Donald R., "Education for Business in Church-Related Liberal Arts Colleges," *Journal of Business Education,* 31: 319, April 1956.

An abstract of an Ed.D. dissertation in which the author attempts to see to what extent church-related liberal arts colleges have become "business oriented."

Lee, Dorothy E., "Historical Development of Business Schools from Colonial Times," *American Business Education Association Yearbook, 1957,* pp. 16-29.

A brief but pointed account of the history of business schools, including reference to the junior college movement.

Marshall, Leon C., "School of Commerce." *In* R. A. Kent (Ed.). *Higher Education in America.* Boston: Ginn and Co., 1930.

A relatively short but well-written early history of business education.

Matherly, Walter J., "The Relationship of the School of Business to the College of Liberal Arts," *American Association of Collegiate Schools of Business, Proceedings of the 19th Annual Meeting,* March, 1937, pp. 5-17.

The Dean of the College of Business Administration, University of Florida (1937), gives an interesting account of how business schools originally developed from liberal arts colleges and economics departments.

Prime, John, "Collegiate Business Education in America," *National Business Education Quarterly,* 21:43-46, October 1953.

The Assistant Dean of the New York University School of Commerce presents a concise history of collegiate business schools, showing how they arose to meet changing social and economic conditions.

Puckett, Cecil, "Business Curriculum Practices on the College and University Level," *American Business Education Association Yearbook,* 4:217-225, 1947.

The author relates past trends in collegiate business education to possible future developments, with references to the role of liberal arts.

Willits, Joseph H., "Business Schools and Training for Public Service," *American Association of Collegiate Schools of Business, Proceedings of the 17th Annual Meeting, April, 1935,* pp. 8-17.

A statement by the former Dean of the Wharton School to the effect that business education, if properly presented, can prepare the student for both business and public service.

B. PUBLICATIONS RELATING TO THE ROLE OF LIBERAL ARTS IN BUSINESS EDUCATION PRIOR TO THE WORLD WAR II (1946) PERIOD

1. BOOKS AND MONOGRAPHS

Bossard, James, and J. Frederick Dewhurst, *University Education for Business*. Philadelphia: University of Pennsylvania Press, 1935.

Written in 1935 this volume remains one of the most comprehensive surveys ever made of business schools. Included are such topics as Organization and Objectives, Opinions of Graduates, Role of Liberal Arts, etc.

Cambridge University Committee, *University Education and Business*. Cambridge, England: Cambridge University Press, 1946.

A monograph indicating that many of the problems confronting American business educators are also present in Great Britain.

Endicott, Frank S., *The Guidance and Counseling of Business Education Students*. Cincinnati, Ohio: South-Western Publishing Co., 1946.

A well-known Director of Placement gives his views on the needs of business as regards the educational background of the student applicant.

Stuart, Henry W., *Liberal and Vocational Studies in the College*. Stanford, Calif.: Stanford University Press, 1918.

A Professor of Philosophy advocates a balanced approach between business and liberal education.

Veblen, Thorstein, *The Higher Learning in America*. New York: B. W. Huebsch, 1918.

A famous social scientist comes up with what may be the most vitriolic attack ever made on the whole idea of business education at the college level.

Wharton Survey Advisory Committee, *A Program for the Wharton School*. Philadelphia: University of Pennsylvania, 1957. (Mimeographed.)

Prepared by a faculty advisory committee, this monograph spells out the objectives of modern business education, with special reference to the role of liberal arts.

2. PERIODICALS AND ARTICLES

Adams, James Truslow, "A Test for American Business," *New York Times Magazine,* January 10, 1937, pp. 1-2, 27.

An exceptionally well written article pointing up the needs and objectives of business, as seen from a pre-World War II perspective.

Aurner, Robert, "Business Communication Courses in the College Business Administration Department," *National Business Education Quarterly,* 15:31-44, December 1946.

A Professor of Business Administration discusses the importance of English and Communications in business education at the college level.

Constitution and Standards for Membership (pamphlet). St. Louis, Mo.: American Association of Collegiate Schools of Business, 1962.

This pamphlet is available at the office of the Executive Secretary, Richard C. Reidenbach, 101 North Skinker, Station No. 24, St. Louis 5, Missouri.

Dale, H. C., "The Responsibilities of Schools of Business Administration to Economic Statesmanship," *American Association of Collegiate Schools of Business, Proceedings of the 19th Annual Meeting,* March 1937, pp. 18-23.

The author takes a broad view of business education, feeling that economic statesmanship, as he puts it, should not be sacrificed for short-term vocational objectives.

Fries, Albert C., "College Training for Business," *Journal of Business Education,* 20:11-12, March 1945.

A brief but pointed account of some of the goals of collegiate training for business.

Griswold, A. W., "Liberal Education is Practical Education," *New York Times Magazine,* p. 13ff, November 29, 1933.

A well known educator demonstrates that in a nearly literal sense, liberal education is the most practical of all forms of education.

Hughes, Eugene H., "The Need for Discovering the Fundamental Bases of Higher Education for Business," *American Business Education Association Yearbook,* 14:55-66, 1957.

The Dean of the College of Business Administration, University of Houston, presents a statement on the development of collegiate business education, some of the criticisms that have been voiced in terms of over-specialization, and the long-range outlook.

Hutchinson, R. M., "Liberal vs. Practical Education," *Rotarian,* 69:14-15, September 1946.

An analysis of some of the issues concerning liberal and specialized education.

Natiens, L. J., "Business Before Culture," *North American Review,* 229:705-713, June 1930.

A critical analysis of certain phases of education. The author, an educator, argues that greater effort be made to put cultural values in the over-all business program.

Nystrom, Paul H., "College Training and the New Deal," *American Association of Collegiate Schools of Business, Proceedings of the 17th Annual Meeting,* April 1935, pp. 20-27.

A Professor of Marketing at Columbia takes a rather dim view of the value of liberal education insofar as it relates to the "major currents of present day life."

Oliver, Robert T., "The Old Dilemma: Vocational Training or Liberal Arts?" *School and Society,* 62:219-220, October 6, 1945.

An attempt to integrate, insofar as goals are concerned, liberal arts and vocational training.

Spencer, William R., "The Plan of the Natural Sciences," *Journal of Business,* 5:52-55, Part 3, October 1932.

The Dean of the School of Business, Chicago University (1932), advocates training in the natural sciences as an aid to business education.

Stevenson, Russell A., "The Proposed Survey of Business Education," *American Association of Collegiate Schools of Business, Proceedings of the 21st Annual Meeting,* April 1939, pp. 8-26.

The Dean of the University of Minnesota's School of Business Administration discussed the results of a questionnaire survey of 35 business schools. Questions related to objectives, role of liberal arts, etc.

————, "The Survey of Schools of Business," *American Association of Collegiate Schools of Business, Proceedings of the 22nd Annual Meeting,* April 1940, pp. 23-29.

The author reports on the results of a questionnaire survey, based on responses by business school graduates. Written English proved to be the most valuable subject taken in college.

————, "The Relationship Between a College of Commerce and a Liberal Arts Division," *American Association of Collegiate Schools of Business, Proceedings of the 23rd Annual Meeting,* May 1941, pp. 65-68.

An outline of some of the more "ideal" relationships between the business school and the liberal arts division of a college or university.

C. PUBLICATIONS RELATING TO THE ROLE OF LIBERAL ARTS
IN COLLEGIATE BUSINESS EDUCATION FROM THE
POST WORLD WAR II PERIOD TO THE PRESENT*

STATEMENTS AND VIEWS OF BUSINESS EDUCATORS

1. PERIODICALS AND ARTICLES

Bangs, F. Kendrick, "Curriculum Revision in Business Education at the
Collegiate Level," *National Business Education Quarterly,* 28: 13-17,
May 1960.

An associate professor of business education, in writing about the business teacher at the college level, feels that the curriculum should include
the three areas of (*a*) liberal education, (*b*) professional education,
and (*c*) specialized education in the field of business for purposes of
teaching emphasis.

Borland, Helen, "Collegiate Business Education Problems," *American
Business Education,* 6:215-220, May 1950.

Feeling that this country faces a danger in reaching for Utopian ideal-
ism, the author spells out the responsibilities of business educators.

Bradley, Joseph F., "The Emergence of Business as a Profession," *Collegiate News and Views,* 11:11-15, March 1958.

A Professor of Finance at Penn State College of Business Administration, the author points out the advisability of business becoming professionalized.

Brown, Courtney, "Business in Cap and Gown," *Saturday Review,*
40:16-18, January 19, 1957.

The Dean of the Graduate School of Business, Columbia University,
points up some of the changing directions in business education, stating
that the latter can be "taught in the great liberal tradition."

————, "Knowledge of What?" *Saturday Review,* 42:52 ff., January
17, 1959.

The Dean of the Graduate School of Business at Columbia University

* Materials include statements and views of educators and business men as well
as the results of surveys and studies. For reader convenience, the publications have
been grouped according to author affiliation: business-educators, non-business educators, and business practitioners.

writes of the growing concern with the patterns of business school curricula, contending that "the task of a business school, and particularly of a graduate business faculty, must be comprehensive if it is to succeed in helping its graduates become balanced and effective members of the business community." Also mentioned is the importance of the attitudes of businessmen on the personal lives of individuals—another reason for the high caliber of business leadership required today.

Cutler, Howard, "Organization of Collegiate Schools of Business," *Collegiate News and Views,* 7:1-8, October 1953.

A survey of 92 business schools showing that in the larger universities departments of economics tend to be located in the College of Liberal Arts, while in universities of less than 15,000 enrollment the economics departments are likely to be a part of the business school.

Dale, E., "Social and Moral Responsibilities of the Executive in the Large Corporation," *American Economic Review: Papers and Proceedings,* 51: 540-563, May 1961.

The subject matter of the article follows closely the title. Corporate relations, according to Professor Dale, are so complex, subtle, and indirect—and so intertwined with the attitudes of both management and stockholders—that it is sometimes easy to avoid the onus of social responsibility.

Davis, Keith, "Human Relations as a Basis," *American Business Education Association Yearbook,* 14:136-149, 1957.

A Professor of Management at the Indiana University School of Business advocates the "human relations" approach to business education, and suggests methods whereby human relations content can fit into the business curriculum.

Fries, Albert, "The Role of Collegiate Institutions in Stimulating Effective Leadership," *National Business Education Quarterly,* 23: 31-33, May 1955.

A discussion of the role of collegiate schools of business in preparing and training business teachers.

Glos, R. E., "The Establishment of Curriculums in Higher Education for Business," *American Business Education Association Yearbook,* 14:153-163, 1957.

The Dean of the School of Business Administration, Miami University, Ohio, discusses some problems—as well as solutions—of business school curriculum building, including the alignment of liberal arts offerings.

Hailstones, T. J., E. E. Roberts, and John Steinbruegee, "Personnel

Managers Evaluate a College Business Program," *Collegiate News and Views,* 8:7-11, May 1955.

A timely and important article reporting questionnaire results showing what kinds of courses *personnel managers* believe to be important.

Hamilton, Herbert A., "The Present Status of Higher Education for Business," *American Business Education Association Yearbook,* 14:30-46, 1957.

The Dean of the College of Commerce, Southwestern Louisiana Institute, places business schools in their present setting, with some discussion of liberal arts or "general" courses as compared with the role of specialized courses.

Hamilton, Roger S., "Business Administration Courses Adjusted to Community Needs," *American Business Education,* 7:281-283, May 1951.

The Dean of Northeastern University's College of Business Administration relates collegiate business training to over-all community needs.

Hurley, Morris E., "Liberal Arts As A Basis," *American Business Education Association Yearbook,* 14:67-78, 1957.

Syracuse University's Dean of the Business College presents a pointed discussion on the need for basing collegiate business training on a foundation of liberal arts.

McPhelin, Rev. Michael, "The Humanities in Education for Business," *Collegiate News and Views,* 8:1-6, October 1954.

A former Dean of Fordham University's School of Business presents a convincing argument to the effect that there is no necessary goal-dichotomy between business and liberal education.

Mee, John F., "Management Philosophy for Professional Executives," *Business Horizons,* pp. 5-11. *Indiana Business Review* supplement, 1956. *[Bloomington: Indiana University, 1956.]*

The Chairman of the Management Department, Indiana University School of Business, spells out the objectives of modern management including that of social responsibility.

Mulcahy, Richard E., "Why a Business College?" *American Review,* 98(14):421-424, January 11, 1958.

The Dean of the College of Business Administration, University of San Francisco, contends that business courses can be liberal rather than vocational, and that the former approach serves the function among other things of high student-motivation.

Nicks, Earl, "Problems of Business Educators in Collegiate Schools of Business," *National Business Education Quarterly,* 20:17-20, May 1952.

A discussion of the importance of providing the proper atmosphere for getting business majors interested in teaching positions.

Olson, Paul, "The Professional Economist and Economic Education," *Collegiate News and Views,* 11:1-6, March 1958.

An economist believes that the teaching of economics should include "the whole area of social studies as well as participation in a formal course bearing the title Economics."

Spengler, Joseph, "An Economist Views Collegiate Business Education," *Collegiate News and Views,* 8:1-3, March 1955.

A Professor of Economics presents his ideas of what constitutes a sound business curriculum.

Taylor, Weldon, "Are Business Schools Meeting the Challenge?" *Collegiate News and Views,* 10:1-6, October 1956.

A well-written article pointing up the requirements of future business leaders and the role of such factors as liberal arts, community responsibility, etc.

Terry, George, "Adjusting the College Curriculum to Demands of the Business Office," *American Business Education,* 8:23-26, October 30, 1951.

A business educator discusses some of the requirements of the modern business office and their effect on the business curriculum.

Tidwell, M. Fred, "The Graduate Business School of Tomorrow," *American Business Education,* 7:212-216, March 1951.

The author believes graduate business education should point toward "mature men who have had actual business experience," and explains his reasons.

Tonne, Herbert A., "How Liberal are the Liberal Arts?" *Journal of Business Education,* 35:248 ff., March 1960.

Tonne, of New York University, feels that the liberal arts are not as "liberal" as they claim to be, and he states that he has "found no relationship between liberalism . . . and formal liberal arts learning." The author concludes that "The needs of the pupil and the way the subject is taught are the criteria in terms of which subject matter should be selected, not personal bias."

Weimer, Arthur N., "Business and General Education," *Business Horizons,* 32:1-6, June 1957.

The Dean of the Business School, Indiana University, gives his views on the relationship between business and general education.

"What Future Executives Must Know," *Nation's Business,* 44:34, August 1956.

In an interview Dean Charles C. Abbott of the Graduate School of Business, University of Virginia, defends the view that business education should aim at developing generalists rather than specialists. He bases his argument on the proposition that the executive of tomorrow will be called on to make increasingly broad decisions.

STATEMENTS AND VIEWS OF NON-BUSINESS EDUCATORS

1. PERIODICALS AND ARTICLES

Baltzell, E. Digby, "Bell Telephone's Experiment in Education," *Harper's,* 210:73-77, March 1955.

A sociologist describes the highly successful executive training program of the Bell Telephone Company, with examples of the specific values of humanistic teaching.

Bolman, F. De W., "Romance Between Colleges and Industry?" *Educational Record,* 36: 150-156, April 1955.

A former President of Franklin and Marshall College comments on what he believes to be a closer relationship between the colleges and the business world.

Brown, Francis J. (Ed.), "Higher Education Under Stress," *The Annals of the American Academy of Political and Social Science,* Vol. 301, September 1955.

This issue of the *Annals* is devoted entirely to the various problems confronting higher education.

Calkins, Robert D., "Liberal Arts in Business Training," *Association of American Colleges Bulletin,* 38:329-335, May 1952.

The Vice President and Director of the General Education Board makes an eloquent plea for the necessity of liberal arts training as it affects business students and future business leaders. The choice is whether the business school is going "to train men for specific jobs in business or whether it is going to train men capable of rising to the responsible positions in business."

————, "Problems of Business Education," *Journal of Business,* 34:1-9, January 1961.

A critical review of the Gordon-Howell and Pierson reports, which notes the neglect in these reports of such things as the growth of "continuing education for business," the needs of non-business administration, and the needs for variety in training.

McCormick, J. P., "The English Major As A Business Man," *College English,* 17:486-487, May 1956.

An academician points out some of the advantages of the English major in the business world.

Murray, E. B., "Business Values of Classical Training," *Classical Journal,* 52:49-53, November 1956.

An eloquent defense of the proposition that classical training has realistic value as collegiate preparation for business.

Norton, K. B., "Latin Major in Industry," *Classical Journal,* 52:13-14, October 1956.

An interesting discussion of some of the ramifications of the effectiveness of the Latin major in industry.

Pamp, F. E., "Liberal Education as Training for Business," *High Points,* 37:5-22, December 1955.

A well written article showing many of the values of liberal and humanistic education as preparation for a career in business and industry.

Williams, Lloyd P., "The Educational Consequences of Laissez Faire," *School and Society,* 85:38-39, February 2, 1957.

The author reviews the status of American education and the extent to which American business ideology and practice have influenced higher education. One of the causes of the failure of our educational system, the author believes, is "the pervasive nature of business acquisitiveness and the measure of efficiency in education by business standards." Furthermore, "insofar as the business ideology fosters a climate of educational opinion that abets materialism, scientism, and the philosophy of immediacy, it debases that which it touches and renders a disservice to humanity."

STATEMENTS AND VIEWS OF BUSINESS LEADERS

1. BOOKS AND MONOGRAPHS

Randall, Clarence M., *A Business Man Looks at Liberal Education.* White Plains, N.Y.: The Adult Education Association, 1956.

Written from the view of the businessman, this volume explores some of the facets of present-day liberal education, including the relation between such education and business, social responsibility, etc.

Shepard, David A., *Liberal Education in an Industrial Society.* Public Affairs Pamphlet No. 248, New York: Public Affairs Committee, 1957, 28 pp.

One of the well known Public Affairs Pamphlets Series, this one is an exceptionally well written account of the need for the liberally trained man in today's industrial society.

2. PERIODICALS AND ARTICLES

Besse, Ralph M., "The Vision of the Future," *Vital Speeches*, 28(18): 551-555, July 1957.

The Vice President of the Cleveland Electric Illuminating Company advocates liberal education as "essential to give the prospective business leader some comprehension of man's relation to man — his psychology, his origins, his understanding, his motivation."

Brown, Courtney, "Human Problems First," *Saturday Review,* 36:3-6, November 21, 1953.

The author suggests four reasons for what he thinks will be a greater attractiveness of liberal arts for business needs: (1) Western traditions; (2) Complexity of business decisions; (3) A need for more and more broad gauge men; (4) A need for self-expression by big business.

Carr, G. G., "New Partnership; Business and Education," *Iron Age,* 178:51-53, September 6, 1956.

A brief but pointed article showing that in the nature of the modern world a closer relationship between business and education is most desirable.

Curtice, H. H., "Industry and Education in a Free Society," *Journal of Higher Education,* 26:357-360, October 1955.

A well known corporation executive gives his views on the relation between business and education within the framework of a democratic society.

"Industry and College: Partners in Development," *Steel,* 139:119-126, November 12, 1956.

An incisive editorial spelling out the growth-relationship between U. S. industry and collegiate education.

Nichols, B. J., "Education for Management Leadership," *Vital Speeches,* 28: 154-157, December 15, 1961.

Nichols, General Manager and Vice President of Dodge (Chrysler) Motor Co., feels that the educational system in the United States should cooperate with the industrial system to develop the management leader of tomorrow. Even the business schools should ". . . encourage *all* of their students to acquire a broad and liberal education." The author goes on to say that "The main object of education is to tap the human potential."

Nickerson, Albert L., "Climbing the Managerial Ladder," *Saturday Review,* 36:38-39, November 21, 1953.

The Vice-President of the Socony-Vacuum Oil Company reports that "Our business system, indeed our whole scheme of contemporary American life, requires the education of young men and women of moral stamina who can think and who can discriminate among values. This implies the necessity for the continued extension of a sound liberal education to every American boy and girl with the capacity to assimilate it."

Shepherd, David, "Management in Search of Men," *Atlantic Monthly,* 197:65-66, March, 1956.

An eloquent presentation of the personnel needs of modern management.

GENERAL

1. BOOKS AND MONOGRAPHS

Carroll, Thomas H. (Ed.), *Business Education for Competence and Responsibility.* Chapel Hill: North Carolina University Press, 1954.

A well-edited volume containing a number of views on business curricula, goals and objectives, and the interaction between general and specialized education.

Copland, Melvin T., *And Mark an Era.* Boston: Little, Brown and Co., 1958, Chs. 1 and 2.

An illuminating account of business school educational policy, with reference to the Harvard program.

Gordon, Robert A., and James E. Howell, *Higher Education for Business.* New York: Columbia University Press, 1959.

The Ford Foundation sponsored study of business education, its problems, and suggestions for remedies. Together with the Pierson study, this is one of the two major surveys of business education in the post World War II period.

Havemann, Ernest, and Patricia West, *They Went to College.* New York: Harcourt, Brace, and Co., 1952.

One of the best surveys of the American college graduate ever made. Chapter Twelve compares the relative "success" (after graduation) of the A. B. and the specialist with some interesting results.

McGrath, Earl J., and Charles H. Russell, *Are Liberal Arts Colleges Becoming Professional Schools?"* New York: Bureau of Publications, Teachers College, Columbia University, 1958.

A provocative account suggesting that some liberal arts colleges have elements of education that more properly belong in the realm of professional training.

Newcomer, Mabel, *The Big Business Executive—The Factors That Made Him, 1900–1950.* New York: Columbia University Press, 1955.

The author surveys the presidents and board chairmen of the largest railroad, public utilities, and industrial organizations as regards traits, percentage attending college, etc.

Pierson, Frank C., *Survey of Business Education Questionnaire: Summary of Preliminary Findings.* New York: sponsored by the Carnegie Corporation, 1958.

A Preliminary Report released in connection with the Carnegie Corporation's survey of business education. Statistical compilations include business school enrollment, size of faculty, types of majors, liberal arts requirements, etc.

———, *The Education of American Businessmen.* New York: McGraw-Hill Book Co., 1959.

A Professor of Economics at Swarthmore College, Pierson has written one of the two major post-war books on business education. The author has many critical comments about the "narrowness" of some programs, and suggests (with concrete examples) curriculum revisions for certain types of business schools.

Silk, Leonard S., *The Education of Businessmen.* New York: Committee for Economic Development, 1960.

A critical and provocative examination of recent thinking about business education in the light of the present-day "market."

Whyte, William H., Jr., *The Organization Man.* Garden City, N.Y.: Doubleday and Co., 1956. See especially Chapters VII and VIII.

Whether or not one agrees with Whyte, this book may well be one of the most important ever written about American business. Chapter Seven is a severe criticism of the "narrowization" of present business curricula, while Chapter Eight criticizes the over-all effect of business on college education.

2. PERIODICALS AND ARTICLES

"Are B-Schools on the Right Track?" *Business Week,* April 13, 1957, p. 50.

A progress report of the two studies carried out through grants from the Ford Foundation and Carnegie Corporation. Goals of the two surveys are discussed, in terms of what is needed for a business career.

Aberle, J., "An Evaluation of a College's Curriculum in Business," *National Business Education Quarterly,* 24:1, October 1955.

An abstract of an Ed. D. thesis which had as its theme the effectiveness of a specific university's business program.

Bailey, Nathan A., "Education for Business Leadership," *Collegiate News and Views,* 13: 15-16, March 1960.

A short but pithy account of what the author feels are some essentials in business education for leadership in present-day society.

Bienvenu, B. J., "Status of Schools of Business Administration in a Changing Society," *Southwestern Social Science Quarterly, 1960 Supplement,* pp. 245-249.

In writing about business schools, Bienvenu feels that they have lowered their standards to ". . . fit the students instead of attempting to raise the students to a higher level." The claim is made that more stress should be given to the study of administration in the business schools, and that the students of business administration ". . . should be required to study with some depth the social sciences and the humanities" if they are to be prepared to deal with the world of ideas.

Brickman, W. W., "Liberal Education and Industrial Leadership," *School and Society,* 85:253-254, September 14, 1957.

A short but pointed article written by the secretary of the above journal and emphasizing the importance of liberal arts content in present-day collegiate business programs.

————, "Liberal Education and Industrial Leadership," *School and Society,* 85: 253, September 14, 1957.

The author contends that present-day industry is a great deal more interested in the liberally educated graduate than heretofore, and that the educational system should take cognizance of this fact. "More emphasis on the educator as a man and less on the educator as a technician would help make the profession of education a more humanistic and consequently a more influential one."

Campbell, William, "Integrating English in Professional Business Courses at the Undergraduate Level," *Collegiate News and Views,* 10:15-19, October 1956.

The author cites a specific example—English—wherein schools of business and liberal arts schools might profitably pool their efforts.

Clark, H., "Education in our Complex Society," *NEA Journal,* April 1962, p. 52.

A brief note pointing out some educational essentials needed in coping with modern, industrialized, complex-type societies.

Compton, Wilson, "Corporation Support," *The Annals of the American Academy of Political and Social Science,* 301:140-147, September 1955.

The President of the Council for Financial Aid to Education presents some figures which show that at present from six to eight per cent of college and university revenue is derived from voluntary financial support by business corporations.

Corrigan, Francis, "Whither Collegiate Business Education?" *School and Society,* 83:45-47, February 1956.

A discussion relative to the future path of American business education. The author raises some interesting points apropos of the "generalist" versus "specialist" argument.

Donovan, T. R., "Socioeconomic and Educational Factors Influencing the Achievement Level of Individuals in Large-Scale Organizations," *Sociology and Social Research,* 46: 416-425, July 1962.

An associate professor of management studies executives in four corporations. Results indicate substantial differences in educational and economic backgrounds as between executives and lower managers. Twice as many lower managers were characterized as having had minimal opportunity as compared with the executives.

Drucker, Peter F., "Graduate Business Schools," *Fortune,* 42:92-94, August 1950.

A pointed critique of professional business education, with special reference to the graduate level.

Endicott, Frank, "An Analysis of Factors Relating to the Employment of College Graduates in Business," *United Business Education Association Forum,* 1:30-32, May 1947.

A factual analysis of some of the curricular factors affecting the employment of business school graduates.

Frank, S., and W. Benton, "Failure of the Business Schools," *Saturday Evening Post,* February 18, 1961, pp. 26ff.

A provocative article, written in popular style, critizing numerous facets of present business school educational programs.

Hansen, Carl W., "Curriculum Practices on the College and University Level," *American Business Education Association Yearbook,* 5:211-216, 1947.

The author believes that "Education has as its fundamental purpose the development and the training of citizens who can live in and contribute to a dynamic society," and that therefore there can "be no real separation of general education and professional education."

Hazard, L., "Humanities for the Businessman," *Harvard Business Review,* 38: 39-44, November 1960.

An account by Professor Hazard of his humanities program for executives at the Carnegie Institute of Technology.

"How to be a Business Man," *Economist,* 184:687-688, August 31, 1957.

The observation is made that business decisions now require training in the academic disciplines, and that the most effective business schools are those post-graduate institutions which accept liberal arts graduates.

Kozelka, Richard, "Professional Education for Business Administration," *Higher Education,* 9:184, April 15, 1953.

A well known business educator presents some views on the objectives of professional business administration programs.

Lockley, Lawrence C., "Business Education and the Humanities," *School and Society,* 5:417-420, December 29, 1951.

The writer states that "Essentially there need be little difference in the substantive content of courses in colleges of liberal arts and in schools of business . . . . Political science, statistics, history . . . sociology . . . these are the foundation of the sound business education. And they are equally appropriate to the college of liberal arts."

Mackay, LaMar, and Donald Bacon, "Are Business Schools Beneficial?" *Wall Street Journal,* March 17, 1958, pp. 1, 11.

Two staff reporters of the Wall Street Journal interview a number of business educators and business leaders and discover that the two groups "split sharply on the value of a business education."

"Management Pattern: Some Trophies from the 'Jungle'," *Business Week,* February 16, 1963, p. 140.

A provocative short-article listing the best management books of 1962, and questioning whether leadership in the management area has "irretrievably passed from the professionals to the educators."

May, F. B., "Business Administration Curricula and the New Research Techniques," *Southwestern Social Science Quarterly,"* 1959 Supplement, pp. 41-48.

An interesting discussion of various quantitative research techniques developed during the post-World War II period.

Mortimer, C. G., "Industry's Stake in Education," *Vital Speeches,* 29: 270-273, February 15, 1963.

The author takes the view that the present-day "stake" of industry in education is indeed a pressing one.

Nelson, C. A., "Liberal Education for Public Service?" *Public Administration Review,* 18: 278-289, Fall, 1958.

The author stresses the need for broadly and adequately trained personnel in the vital area of public service.

"New Look in Business Schools—Stanford's B-School." *Business Week,* June 17, 1961, pp. 156-158ff.

An extensive review of the vast changes that have occurred in Stanford's business school curriculum under the direction of Dean Ernest Arbuckle, former president of W. R. Grace and Co., who believes that "The time is past when business schools can be content to follow. We must anticipate business trends by giving our students the intellectual tools they will need five, ten, or more years from now."

Odiorne, G. S., "Uneasy Look at College Recruiting," *Vital Speeches,* 28: 60-63, November 1, 1961.

Dr. Odiorne, Professor of Industrial Relations at the University of Michigan, writes of the "lapse in understanding" which exists between the university placement director and the corporation recruiter in regard to college recruiting. He suggests that the recruiters might attempt to give the student a wider range of literature on the corporation before an interview is set up, while the placement officers ". . . might turn their efforts toward communicating the world of business and the corporation to the students and faculty with . . . more skill."

Patterson, W. D., "Business: Our Newest Profession," *Saturday Review,* 40:28ff, January 19, 1957.

The Associate Publisher of the *Saturday Review* notes with satisfaction that business training in the vocational sense is being superseded by professional training "in which the subject is related in meaningful terms to the basic liberal tradition of learning."

Peck, Maynard, "Business Education in the Liberal Arts College," *Association of American Colleges Bulletin,* 41:297-302, May 1955.

The Head of the Department of Economics and Business, Sterling College, believes that highly specialized business programs have not proved themselves and that the graduates "were poorly prepared to meet the real life problems as encountered in the business world." The writer believes strongly in collegiate business education but only in terms of a liberal arts synthesis.

"Popularity Swamps Business Schools," *Business Week,* December 15, 1956, pp. 193-194.

It is contended that business schools are generally moving toward broadening the educational base and reducing specialization; however, the writer states that there is little agreement as to just what this means, in terms of the curriculum.

Robinson, Marshall A., "The Academic Content of Business Education," *Journal of Higher Education,* 33(3): 131-140, March 1962.

An account of the move to higher-level graduate business education at the University of Pittsburgh.

Sarah, Sister M., "The Liberal Arts vs. Specialized Education," *Journal of Business Education,* 35: 350-51, May 1960.

In regard to the ever-present conflict between liberal versus specialized education, the author feels that both have distinctive values and that both are necessary for the needs of modern living. She advocates that a balance be achieved between the two in order to turn out "cultured and competent citizens of a democratic society . . ." Such a balance would provide for both a "liberally educated and astute businessman."

"Should a Business Man be Educated?" *Fortune,* 45:113-114, April 1953.

A Fortune editorial wherein some of the blame for over-specialization in business education is placed on the business firm.

Stout, Edward, "University Training for Business, *Collegiate News and Views,* 10:9-12, December 1956.

The Registrar of De Paul University would like to see business schools move away from the how-to-do-it orientation. Ideas for a more effective business curriculum are presented.

Thompson, Willard, "Critics Challenge College Business Programs," *California Business Education Association Bulletin,* 17: 1ff., May 1960.

A brief account of the recent surveys of collegiate business education. Following these surveys, similar-type statements were published in any number of business and educational journals.

Whyte, William H., Jr., "The New Illiteracy," *Saturday Review,* 36:33-35, November 21, 1953.

This short article contains some of the points made in *The Organization Man,* although stated in somewhat different form. Whyte doubts that a genuine revival of interest in the humanities and liberal arts is forthcoming.

Wingate, John W., "The Question of Business Specialization in Colleges and Universities," *Collegiate News and Views,* 13: 1-6, May 1960.

Another viewpoint is given regarding the issue of the role of educational specialization in American colleges and universities.